*Protecting your family's wealth
from predatory taxes.*

Timothy J. Kissling, CPA

Huston Publishing LTD

ISBN 978-0-9914102-0-0

Huston Publishing, Ltd.

Printed in the United States of America

Think Beyond Tax Now

*Protecting your family's wealth
from predatory taxes.*

TABLE OF CONTENTS

Foreword

Foreword

When Tim Kissling asked me to contribute the foreward for his *Think Beyond Tax Now* book, I was delighted. I have worked with many tax advisors over the years, and from the very beginning of our relationship several years ago, Tim stood out. It's rare to find a tax advisor who has the skill of a craftsman, the precision of an engineer, and the ability to explain complex concepts in a way that makes them seem simple and intuitive. This book is an outgrowth of, and an expression of, Tim's talents.

In tax planning, the approach of a craftsman is paramount. Its not just about knowing the tools; its about knowing how to use and apply the tools. Only a craftsman can properly mold the complex tax code around the specific nuances of your situation, in order to create the lowest possible tax liability. In the hands of a craftsman like Tim, effective tax planning could quite literally change your lifestyle.

In tax planning, the precision of an engineer is also needed, in order to deploy tax strategies in a way that fully conforms with – and fully leverages – the tax code. Tax planning is not difficult if the only thing you are doing to reduce your taxes is deducting mortgage interest. However, if you are a business owner who is confronted with a myriad of more complex tax planning options, precision is important. A tax planning strategy, if used with precision, can create meaningful tax reductions. The opposite is also true. When taking your tax planning to the next level, you need someone with Tim's experience and acumen in your corner.

Perhaps most importantly, Tim's fluency in his craft enables him to explain tax law in a way that clarifies rather than confuses, and in a way that simplifies rather than stymies. Tim leaves the complexity where it belongs – in the tax code. He leaves you, as a business owner, with understanding and confidence that you really can exert a significant amount of control over your largest single expense.

As far as Tim is concerned, the Internal Revenue Code is what defines the size and shape of the playing field. However, it does not control the outcome of the game. You do - based on choices that you make. That playing field is governed by 71,684 pages of rules in the tax code (up from "only" 16,845 pages in 2006) that determine what will appear on the "Amount You Owe" line of your Form 1040. As a taxpayer, you can choose to use the entire playing field and use as many rules to your advantage as possible, or you can choose to limit yourself to using only some of the rules. Consider the possibility – indeed, accept the reality – that you have only been using some of the rules in your favor, and are therefore probably overpaying your taxes.

Tim wants business owners to take control of their financial future. He wants you to think beyond where your business is today, and think about where you want to take your business and your family's financial security in the future. Every business owner needs to have a financial plan, and that plan needs to take into account and fully integrate tax planning. Not just income taxes, but other taxes that you will eventually face. If you don't take control of your financial future now, the IRS will be able to take control on your behalf in the future.

I believe you will enjoy Tim's insights. It will be thought provoking. It will challenge your previous notions about whether or not you really are "doing everything you can to reduce your taxes." My hope for you is that you will make the decision to **Think Beyond Now™**, and take action that will enable you to enhance your family's financial security.

> Dr. David Runge
> Managing Partner
> Tax Law Solutions, LLC

"There are two systems of taxation in our country: one for the informed and one for the uninformed." **Learned Hand,** *Judge, United States Court of Appeals for the Second Circuit.*

Preface

Preface

As I start to study my clients and what we have been able to accomplish with them over the last several years I have found a commonality among the group.
T.K.

So, you decided to pick up the book. You wanted to check it out and find out what in the world is the **Kissling Tax Method™**. Well, my first question is: why in the world would you want to read a book written by a CPA? You either have a very boring life, or you have hit the point where you are fed up with your annual income tax bill and you want to find a better way to save taxes. I hope it is the latter.

In my 30-year career as both a CPA and a financial planner, I have had the privilege of working with really great people.

As I reflect on my career, I see many people who taught me to be a better auditor, tax preparer and tax planner.

I grew into a more relational rather than transactional adviser as several top level partners at some CPA firms poured their hearts into making me a better manager of people and a better manager of the financial needs of my clients.

My only regret is not appreciating their efforts at that time.

Then, I think about the many types of clients. What opportunities! Sometimes I wonder how I ended up with such a diverse group.

I believe I have worked with just about every kind of client. I have worked with individuals who were not necessarily blessed with a lot of financial wealth, but who possessed hearts of gold.

I have worked with both "mom and pop" companies as well as companies owned by some of the wealthiest individuals in the

United States. I have also worked with companies that are so small I wondered why they were in business at all.

On the other hand, I have worked with companies that have sales in the billions of dollars. In 2012 my firm prepared tax returns for clients in over 35 states. What a blessing my career has been.

As I start to study my clients and what we have been able to accomplish with them over the last several years, I have found a commonality among the group with certain issues that I deal with on a regular basis. Issues that are common to business owners regardless of their size.

You see, I don't view my clients simply as the contractors, doctors, lawyers, financial advisors or merchandisers they are. I view them as entrepreneurs who are in just in one business: **the business of building wealth**.

One of my discoveries over the years is that the "American Way" teaches us all to focus on how much money we earn. We fit into a natural pecking order based upon our annual income. The more you make; the better society tends to treat you. Our children go off to college focusing on the career opportunities that match their personalities and their personal financial goals.

They go to college in an effort to enhance their earning potential. But, I have never seen a child leave for college with the goal of learning how to build wealth. Wealth and income are two completely different concepts, and I don't think that class can be found in any course catalog.

Here's the big secret. The concept of building wealth is actually very simple. It is so simple I will let you in on the secret right now. Get out your highlighter, because here it is: To build wealth, all you have to do is spend less money than you make.

To build lots of wealth all you have to do is spend a lot less than what you earn.

One of our challenges as entrepreneurs is in controlling our costs. Generally, within our individual industries, if we can control our costs and we can control our bottom line, then we stand a good chance to build wealth.

I see contractors negotiating better deals for materials. I watch manufacturers controlling their labor hours. But the situation I see more than anything else is entrepreneurs who do everything possible to increase sales and reduce costs, and then they show up at their CPA's office and ask him to "figure out what the tax bite is going to be."

This may be your biggest expense, and it only gets a limited focus of your time! You see, most CPA's are good at figuring out what your tax liability is going to be. They might have a few small tricks to shift your income from this year to next year.

Maybe even defer the taxable income for a few years. But the vast majority of CPA's simply figure out the tax. They tell you they are tax planners, but the truth is, they are tax figurers.

For most companies, your income tax expense is your biggest expense. With the latest income tax law changes, your income tax expense could be almost 50% of your earnings. Frankly, with 50% of your net income being taken by our federal, state, and local governments, it is going to be more difficult to build wealth today than it has been in the last 25 years.

With this in mind, I set out to develop the "Kissling Tax Method™." The Kissling Tax Method™ is a process. It is not a specific tool. It is a tax savings strategy that has been developed in an effort to substantially reduce income taxes on a long-term and permanent basis. It is how I can assist my clients to maximize their wealth by reducing their federal, state and local tax liabilities on both a current and long-term basis.

To build wealth you need to take a long-term methodical approach. You need to have a plan. You have to think beyond your current year's tax bill. You have to look at your long-term life goals. You need to **"Think Beyond Now™."**

> *"What at first was plunder assumed the softer name of revenue."* **Thomas Paine**

Introduction

...to help you to better comprehend how the tactics and methods I put into practice on a daily basis as a financial advisor can help you, too. **T.K.**

I am going to introduce you to a cast of characters and their stories; these stories reflect the real life stories of my clients over the years. In my business, confidentiality is key, so I have written this book with composite stories involving the individuals who have lived these scenarios, to help you to better comprehend how the tactics and methods I put into practice on a daily basis as a financial advisor can help you, too.

You will meet people like Fred, the owner of a toothpick company, or Tony, the self-made millionaire construction guy. Dan and Rachel, who have been married, started a business, raised a family and eventually faced their retirement years. Then there's Joe whose employees desire retirement plans, and he has to face how to go about providing for himself and his family as well as for his employees.

Their stories are your stories, because as entrepreneurs, you all have in common the drive and passion to grow your business successfully, and to acquire a high quality of life for yourselves and your families.

Follow me as I weave their stories, their choices for good or bad, throughout this book. As we uncover some of the secrets to successfully mitigating tax liabilities, and even discovering methods for tax-free retirement and estate planning.

———— ❧ ————

"If Thomas Jefferson thought taxation without representation was bad, he should see how it is with representation." **Rush Limbaugh**

1

A Brief History of Taxes

There are days when I feel convinced that taxes were the first evil brought to the world. **T.K.**

Taxes have been a controversial subject for centuries, with a reputation that reaches Biblical proportions. In fact, there are days when I feel convinced that taxes were the first evil brought to the world by Satan after the fall of man. Perhaps, as a business owner, you share in this conviction.

As Jennifer Rosenberg mentions in her article "History of Income Tax in the U.S.," the first known, written record of taxes dates back to ancient Egypt. The author notes that Egyptians were not the only ancient people to hate tax collectors. Ancient Sumerians had a proverb: "You can have a lord, you can have a king, but the man to fear is the tax collector!"

In fact, a history of taxes is a history of the civilization of the world. Major events in our history books were directly related to major tax events.

The ancient Egyptians had their harsh methods, and during the Roman occupation of Israel, Mary and Joseph were famously required to register in Bethlehem. Don't forget the notoriously defiant ride of Lady Godiva, or the world's most famous tea party that took place in Boston Harbor in 1773. The colonists were protesting King George's practice of "taxation without representation."

In fact, a history of taxes is a history of the civilization of the world.

It is common knowledge that taxation and its disturbing relationship with the populace has been a global theme for centuries. The earliest days of our own country began with a large national debt incurred from the revolution that was a reaction to unfair taxation. Nevertheless, Alexander Hamilton, the first U.S. treasurer, institutionalized a form of taxation in order to pay down the national debt.

The 16ᵗʰ Amendment to the Constitution of the United States

The Congress shall have the power to lay and collect taxes on incomes, from whatever source derived, without apportionment among the several States, and without regard to any census or enumeration.

INFORMATION EXCERPTED FROM MILESTONE DOCUMENTS IN THE NATIONAL ARCHIVES [WASHINGTON, DC: NATIONAL ARCHIVES AND RECORDS ADMINISTRATION, 1995] PP. 69–73.)

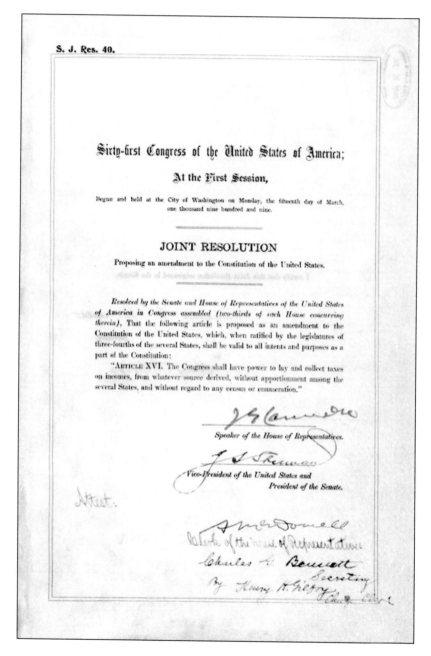

16TH AMENDMENT TO THE U.S. CONSTITUTION:
FEDERAL INCOME TAX (1913)

TO BE FILLED IN BY COLLECTOR.	Form 1040.	TO BE FILLED IN BY INTERNAL REVENUE BUREAU.

INCOME TAX.

List No. ....

.... District of ....

Date received ....

THE PENALTY
FOR FAILURE TO HAVE THIS RETURN IN THE HANDS OF THE COLLECTOR OF INTERNAL REVENUE ON OR BEFORE MARCH 1 IS $20 TO $1,000.
(SEE INSTRUCTIONS ON PAGE 4.)

File No. ....

Assessment List ....

Page .... Line ....

UNITED STATES INTERNAL REVENUE.

RETURN OF ANNUAL NET INCOME OF INDIVIDUALS.

(As provided by Act of Congress, approved October 3, 1913.)

RETURN OF NET INCOME RECEIVED OR ACCRUED DURING THE YEAR ENDED DECEMBER 31, 191....

(FOR THE YEAR 1913, FROM MARCH 1, TO DECEMBER 31.)

Filed by (or for) .... of ....
(Full name of individual.)   (Street and No.)

in the City, Town, or Post Office of .... State of ....
(Fill in page 2 and 3 before making entries below.)

1. GROSS INCOME (see page 2, line 12) .... $..............

2. GENERAL DEDUCTIONS (see page 3, line 7) .... $..............

3. NET INCOME .... $..............

Deductions and exemptions allowed in computing income subject to the normal tax of 1 per cent.

4. Dividends and net earnings received or accrued, of corporations, etc., subject to like tax. (See page 2, line 11).......... $..........

5. Amount of income on which the normal tax has been deducted and withheld at the source. (See page 2, line 9, column A)..

6. Specific exemption of $3,000 or $4,000, as the case may be. (See Instructions 3 and 19) ....

Total deductions and exemptions. (Items 4, 5, and 6) .... $..........

7. TAXABLE INCOME on which the normal tax of 1 per cent is to be calculated. (See Instruction 3). $..........

8. When the net income shown above on line 3 exceeds $20,000, the additional tax thereon must be calculated as per schedule below:

					INCOME.	TAX.
1 per cent on amount over $20,000 and not exceeding $50,000....					$..........	$..........
2	"	"	50,000	"	"	75,000....		
3	"	"	75,000	"	"	100,000....		
4	"	"	100,000	"	"	250,000....		
5	"	"	250,000	"	"	500,000....		
6	"	"	500,000					

Total additional or super tax .... $..........

Total normal tax (1 per cent of amount entered on line 7).... $..........

Total tax liability... $..........

FIRST PAGE OF INCOME TAX FORM 1040,
FROM THE UNITED STATES INTERNAL
REVENUE BUREAU, 1913.

This opened a Pandora's box that has never been closed. Less than a hundred years later, the Civil War was funded with the first income tax (a 3% rate at that time) via a "temporary measure" entitled The Revenue Act of 1862. By the beginning of the last century, we saw the establishment of the income tax and ratification of the 16th Amendment. As Jennifer Rosenberg expresses it, "Also in 1913, the first Form 1040 was created."

Tax Documents and Documentation.

Passed by Congress on July 2, 1909, and ratified February 3, 1913, the 16th amendment established Congress's right to impose a federal income tax.

Considering this long history of taxes, it is reasonable to acknowledge that every government requires money to function, so consequently it needs a means to collect those funds or taxes. We understand the reality that in order to have a fully functioning society, we need a fully functioning government to provide military and police for our security as well as infrastructure and other basic systems for economic development and well-being.

It is a logical conclusion that if a functioning government is required, it is also necessary to pay for that government. As the government grows older, bigger and more costly, one question looms ominously: "Who is going to pay for this government?"

According to a quick online visit to Wikipedia: "Today the IRS collects over $2.4 trillion each tax year from around 234 million tax returns."

There are numerous methods governments use to generate revenue. When viewed together as an entity, federal, state, and local government agencies reveal that our government is expert in the art of collecting revenue.

As a resident of Pennsylvania, I can produce the following list of taxes just off the top of my head: federal, state, and local income taxes;

state sales taxes; federal and state gasoline taxes; real estate taxes at the county, school, and township levels; business privilege tax or local gross receipts tax; and Federal excise taxes.

And the list goes on. . .

> *...it is my opinion that taxation, regardless of the taxation method, is always a political tool.*

In addition to the myriad of taxes levied in my home state of Pennsylvania, our government is masterful at generating revenue through the non-tax taxes that are called "fees and fines."

As citizens, we participate in any number of activities for which our government finds it necessary to require us to have a license or a permit. These include everyday activities like driving a car or improving our homes, which require driver's licenses and building permits.

I know that as a business owner, you can produce many other examples.

From our vantage point, it is clear that taxes have been despised by the masses for as long as they have existed. In addition, it is my opinion that taxation, regardless of the taxation method, is always a political tool.

Let's face it: those who have greater political pull will pay less in taxes than those with less political pull in any given political environment.

This leads us into a brief lesson about the workings of the economy in this country.

> "Our new Constitution is now established, and has an appearance that promises permanency; but in this world nothing can be said to be certain, except death and taxes." **Benjamin Franklin,** in a letter to Jean-Baptiste LeRoy, 1789.

2
The Economy as We Know It

Historically, when a government freely prints its currency, its currency eventually becomes worthless, and the government and related economy fails. **T.K.**

W ill Rogers, the humorist, has received credit for telling the world that "We will always have two things: inflation and taxes." I don't know if he really was the first to say it, but he is in the company of many wise observers who have said it. And he certainly was correct.

What I have found is that most people simply do not understand the concept of either inflation or taxes. Without understanding the basics of inflation and taxation, it is impossible to truly understand how the U. S. economy inevitably will have a direct effect on our ultimate goal of building wealth for our families.

> *The U.S. government has borrowed in excess of $17,000,000,000,000.*

America is at a defining moment.
It seems like America is at a crossroads. The government has borrowed in excess of $17,000,000,000,000. This is not a typographical error.

This is what $17 trillion looks like. Our leaders are continuing to add to the national debt at a staggering rate (more than a trillion dollars per year.)

Furthermore, in 2012 the federal government collected more taxes than ever. Many of our leaders are complaining that the government needs to collect even more taxes. It seems the government is like a growing teenager that you can't feed enough. Our elected officials have one program after another that requires more and more of our money. Let's be honest: you and I both know that no matter what our leaders say, they are not going to stop spending beyond their means.

The government only has so many resources that it can tap for its financial fuel.
First, the government can turn to the taxpayers for more taxes. This is taking place currently with the passing of "American Tax Relief Act of 2013." This piece of legislation that was signed into law in January 2013 did give relief to middle and lower income earners, but also resulted in a significant tax increase on wealthier individuals.

Did you know that the "Obamacare" legislation created about 20 new taxes?

Another concern for wealthier individuals lies in the fact that starting in 2013, the federal government will net a significant increase in tax revenues due to the many new taxes created with Obamacare (officially called the Patient Protection and Affordable Care Act.) Did you know that the Obamacare legislation created about 20 new taxes? Some of the taxes are income related and some are sales related, such as taxes on medical devices and tanning salons.

A second source for revenue is when our federal government simply borrows more money from its citizens, foreign individuals, and foreign governments. This is currently happening at a staggering rate.

Our government has been able to keep the borrowing game going because lenders, private citizens and foreign governments still believe that the United States' government is a good financial risk, in comparison to other alternatives.

Lastly, our government has the ability to print more money. This also is going on right now. The Federal Reserve is printing the money, and then lending it to the federal government.

The Federal Reserve calls this "Quantitative Easing." I call that a fancy, modern phrase for **printing money.**

ASIDE ON THE FED:

THE PRIVATE BANK CALLED THE FEDERAL RESERVE (FED), WHICH MOST PEOPLE THINK IS PART OF THE FEDERAL GOVERNMENT, HAS A GREAT GIG.

IT PRINTS MONEY, PULLING MONEY FROM THIN AIR, AND THEN IT TURNS AROUND AND LOANS MONEY TO THE FEDERAL GOVERNMENT.

SO, THE FEDERAL GOVERNMENT PAYS INTEREST PAYMENTS TO THE FEDERAL RESERVE ON MONEY THAT IS NOT REAL. THE MONEY IS MADE UP FROM THIN AIR AT ZERO COST. I DEDUCE THAT THE FEDERAL RESERVE IS EARNING A PRETTY GOOD PROFIT MARGIN.

I AM NOT GOING TO SPEND TOO MUCH OF OUR TIME GETTING SIDE-TRACKED BY POLITICS OR HOW THE FEDERAL RESERVE CONTROLS OUR ECONOMY, BUT IT IS ESSENTIAL TO KNOW THAT THE DYSFUNCTIONAL RELATIONSHIP OUR GOVERNMENT HAS WITH THE FEDERAL RESERVE WILL EVENTUALLY HAVE A REAL EFFECT ON OUR WEALTH.

Putting economic reality into perspective.
Let's look at how all governments manage the revenue side of their financial operations. It is the economic reality of all governments, not just the United States. Our leaders turn first to taxation. When they cannot generate enough revenue from taxes, they turn to borrowing.

Historically, governments are initially forced to borrow money as a result of a national disaster, such as war, that they cannot manage through normal tax collections. In fact, believe it or not, the U. S. Government borrowed money to support the Revolutionary War. The reality is that the U.S. has had deficits from its beginning.

When a country is no longer able to generate enough revenue from the combination of taxes and borrowing, its government will resort to conjuring money from thin air.

There are several obvious problems with the government's financial equation. (And we won't even take into account the fact that the government created the need for all of this money because it is spending more than it can generate.)

PROBLEM #1: Our leaders know that it is better to tax than to print.
With the government collecting more taxes than ever, it will still focus on creating new taxes, especially new taxes on business owners, because that is currently considered to be politically correct.

PROBLEM #2: Debt disguises problems.
Most business owners clearly understand this. When business owners have lenders who are willing to loan what seems like unlimited amounts of money, it is easy to spend a little wildly.
We just experienced this with the real estate bubble. Banks were willing to loan, and consumers were willing to borrow, knowing that there was a real chance that they could never pay back the debt to the bank.

It is my opinion that the government has been living in the same bubble: institutional investors and foreign governments have been freely lending to the U.S. government for several generations. With open lending, our leaders have been willing to take the loans without a clear method of ever repaying the debt. Investors still seem to believe that the U.S. government is a reasonably safe borrower, despite its shortcomings.

In 2008, as the stock market was crashing, the real estate market was falling apart, and unemployment was going through the roof, investors were buying 30-year treasuries at zero interest. As crazy as it seems, the investors felt that lending money at zero interest (which guarantees a loss to inflation) was a better investment than the stock market, or other foreign debt.

Based upon that, I figure there will still be parties willing to loan the federal government money for a long time, and the fiscal bubble will just grow larger.

PROBLEM #3: Freely printing money can lead to worthless money.
Historically, when a government freely prints money the money eventually becomes worthless and the government and related economy fails. Printing money eventually leads to significant inflation.

Inflation: cause and effect.
I find that most people really don't understand inflation. I hear people making comments that the price of gas has gone up, therefore,

we must have inflation. Or, they complain about the higher price of groceries and they conclude there must be inflation. These are symptoms of inflation. They are not the cause of inflation. Inflation is purely caused by the increase in the amount of money in the economy.

A basic lesson in inflation.
If our economy only traded apples, we produced 10 apples per year, and we had a total of $100 in our economy, then each apple would be worth $10.

If the government decided to add $100 to the economy by printing money, we would have $200, but the same 10 apples. Thus, each apple's worth would inflate to $20.

As you see, the apples' increase in value is the **result or effect** of inflation, not the **cause** of inflation.

Now that you understand that inflation is caused by an increase in the supply of money (or in this case, apples), let's take a more serious look at the United States' economy.

There are several ways to control the supply of money. First, the Federal Reserve can increase the supply by printing money and lending the money to banks and to the government.

By lowering the interest rates they charge the banks and government, the Federal Reserve introduces this money into the economy. Second, banks can increase money in the economy by lending to businesses and consumers.

The opposite is also true. The Federal Reserve can decrease the supply of money by raising interest rates and slowing down the rate in which they lend money. Banks can also slow down the rate in which they lend money. When the supply of money is constricted, we have deflation.

Americans know that the Federal Reserve is printing money at a staggering rate, and the federal government is borrowing enough money to deficit spend in excess of $1 trillion per year. Knowing this to be true, we would expect to see an increase in the inflation rate. But so far we have not.

> *The opposite is also true... when the supply of money is constricted, we have deflation.*

Try to follow this explanation.
The reason we have not seen this increased inflation rate is that since the financial crisis of 2008, banks have reduced lending at a rate close to the rate that the money supply has been expanded by the Federal Reserve.

Think about how banks have reduced lending. It seems that everyone knows someone who has lost a house because his or her mortgage was under water.

How many people had their credit card limit or line of credit limit reduced because the banks needed to cut back on their lending? The reason is that the lenders basically ran out of money to lend in 2008. And, their resources continue to be limited today.

I have clients who are participating in partnerships that are in the business of lending money to business operations that are themselves

Many experts talk as if it is imminent that the Federal Reserve will stop printing money. I contend that the Fed will not be able to stop printing money.

experiencing difficulty in getting loans from banks today. The irony is that the businesses are worthy borrowers who are willing to pay premiums to private lenders to expand their businesses.

Some may argue that Ben Bernanke got it right. They say the government needed to print money and increase the supply of money to offset the pull back from the banks. Well, I hope he is right. Even so, we have to ask: how long can it last?

Banks are businesses.

Banks make money by charging interest on loans. If the banks are not lending money, they are not making money. Eventually they will need to start lending. When that happens, together with the Federal Reserve printing money, the supply of money will expand and we will be faced with new inflation.

Many experts talk as if it is imminent that the Federal Reserve will stop printing money. I contend that the Fed will not be able to stop printing money.

Historical examples of hyperinflation.

History shows us that most governments that cannot control their spending cannot stop printing money once the printing presses get started. Following are a couple of good examples:

German Papiermark.

We have the example of the German government after World War I. In 1922, the largest denomination of the Papiermark was 50,000. A year later it was 100 trillion. This means that by December 1923, the exchange rate with the U.S. Dollar was 4.2 trillion to 1. It is estimated that by November 1923, the yearly inflation rate was considered 325,000,000%.

Peruvian Currency.

During the 1980's, Peru, like many Latin American countries, introduced a number of trade liberalization polices. At the same time, government increased public spending, privatized enterprise, and neglected to service the nation's external debt. As a result, by the end of the 1990's, Peru's already small economy was experiencing not only negative economic growth, but also deficits of all types, as well as hyperinflation.

When hyperinflation became apparent, the Peruvian government replaced the Peru "Old" Sol with the Inti in 1985, at a rate of 1,000 to 1. The largest denomination of this new currency was a 1,000 Inti note. By September 1988, monthly inflation increased by a rate of 132%, and 400% by September 1990. In order to facilitate the new, higher prices of goods and services, new notes were introduced such as the 10,000,000 Inti note by 1991.

Again, the Peruvian government decided to replace the currency, this time with the Nuevo Sol, at a rate of 1,000,000,000 to 1. The result was a currency that was worth one billion times that of only six years before!

As we **Think Beyond Now™**, and focus on our main business of building wealth, we need to challenge ourselves to make sure we are ready for inflation when it appears. If you are in business, you must be adaptable. It is crucial that you position yourself to raise prices to cover your increasing costs. Otherwise, you must find a way to reduce your costs so that you can continue to compete.

*As we **Think Beyond Now™**... we need to challenge ourselves to make sure we are ready for inflation when it appears.*

The fallacy of higher tax brackets.
We must plan so we are prepared to handle the additional tax burden that will come with inflation. As we encounter inflation, we will also inflate into higher tax brackets. At first we will feel good about ourselves because we are "making more money."

What we will discover is that when adjusted for inflation, we will not necessarily be making more money, but rather, because of that inflation, we will be paying more income taxes.

Now, one could argue that many of our tax brackets, tax rates and deductions are adjusted for inflation. However, they are not all adjusted for inflation. Let's not forget that the government controls the calculation of the inflation rate.

The government will always take advantage of inflation to collect more taxes. We need to make sure we plan around that.

When it comes to our investments, it is important to focus on areas that will protect us against inflation. Typically, we look for investment vehicles that have hard assets to support their values. Some of these include equipment leasing, real estate, and certain commodities. We need assets that will grow at a faster rate than inflation, or we will be simply slipping backwards.

To summarize, I think Will Rogers was right. We had better plan for the inflation pressures that are just over the horizon. They are a result of our government's spending ways, mixed with the inability of the government to collect taxes at a rate sufficient to cover the increased spending. Our leaders will continue to look for ways to increase our tax burden. They really don't have much choice.

We cannot fight the government's desire to increase taxes. We will always lose that fight. We are left with no choice but to find ways to fight the tax increases by diving into the tax code and finding the legal tax deductions (that so many people are missing), to reduce our income tax liability.

> *"I traveled the state of Florida for two years campaigning. I have never met a job creator who told me that they were waiting for the next tax increase before they started growing their business. I've never met a single job creator who's ever said to me I can't wait until government raises taxes again so I can go out and create a job."* **Marco Rubio**

3
Why Business Owners Overpay Taxes

I see my job as a retirement planner being to help my clients build their financial assets to a level that will provide them the cash flow necessary to support their desired lifestyle in the later years of their lives. **T.K.**

A s a business owner, here's a question you may never have considered: Why do most business owners overpay their income taxes?

There are multiple answers to this question. Some answers are simple and easy, but others are very complicated.

The first and most prevailing answer is that the Internal Revenue Code is too complicated for most people to figure out. Thus, people err on the side of paying too much rather than risk future audits and possible fines.

The Code is very large and complicated. I find it interesting (if not amusing), that Googling "how many pages are in the Internal Revenue Code" on the Internet does not produce a definite answer. And I thought Google knew everything!

In 2010, there were 71,684 pages in the Internal Revenue Code.

IN A NOVEMBER 2011 ARTICLE IN THE WEEKLY STANDARD, JOHN MCCORMACK WROTE ABOUT THE SIZE OF GENERAL ELECTRIC'S 2010 FEDERAL TAX RETURN.

WISCONSIN CONGRESSMAN PAUL RYAN RELATED HIS CONVERSATION AT A TOWN HALL MEETING.

"I ASKED THE G.E. TAX OFFICER, 'HOW LONG WAS YOUR TAX FORM?' RYAN SAID. "HE SAID, 'WELL, WE FILE ELECTRONICALLY, WE DON'T MEASURE IN PAGES.'"

RYAN ASKED FOR AN ESTIMATE, WHICH CAME BACK AT A STUNNING 57,000 PAGES. ACCORDING TO MCCORMACK, "WHEN RYAN RELATED THE STORY AT THE TOWN HALL MEETING IN JANESVILLE, THERE WERE AUDIBLE GASPS FROM THE CROWD." IF 57,000 PAGES WERE PRINTED OUT IN HARD COPY, IT WOULD CREATE A STACK 19 FEET HIGH!

According to Wiki.answers.com:
In 2006 there were 16,845 pages in the Internal Revenue Code. In 2010 there were 71,684 pages. With over 70,000 pages, how can we expect anyone to understand it all?

Quite frankly, it can simply be overwhelming!

Additional answers to my earlier question.
I find it ironic that in order to deal with a tax code that governs the calculation of the largest personal expense that most people face, most people approach this problem by means of some combination of the following:

1. Allow the enforcer of the rules to explain the rules.
Just think about it: in order to figure out how to prepare our tax returns, we use the literature that is provided by the IRS to explain to us how to give our money to the IRS. It sure is nice of them to summarize their rules for our convenience!

2. Perennial seminar attendance.
"We attend seminars and classes in attempt to glean a better understanding of the rules and regulations." I hear that a lot from clients. The problem with this approach is that most seminars only teach what the IRS rules and regulations are; they don't tell us how to use the rules to our advantage.

3. Family and friends approach.
Another response I often hear is: "We go to our friends and family for advice." Your brother-in-law may be a great guy and a fantastic plumber, but is he really the person you need to advise you on preparing your taxes if he has never even prepared his own income tax form before?

4. Hire an expert.
This assumes that the expert has read the rules and regulations (and of course the expert hasn't), or at least taken sufficient continuing education courses to fully understand the latest rules.

Added to all the above approaches, each person influences his or her actions with a personal sense of right and wrong, based upon personal experience and upbringing.

Mixing in one's personal sense of morality only clouds and inhibits the ability of the taxpayer to adequately analyze and assess liabilities.

First and foremost, it is crucial to understand that tax rules and regulations are about legalities, not moralities. If you calculate your taxes by moralities, you can be sure you will be overpaying your taxes.

If you calculate your taxes by moralities, you can be sure that you will be overpaying your taxes.

The truth of the matter is that everyone assumes that the process of calculating income tax liability is a black and white calculation. In reality, the calculation starts with facts that have already been warped with assumption and interpretation. In other words, accounting is an art, not a science.

Let's take a look at basic decisions that have an effect on calculating your tax liability.

To get started, as a business owner, you first need to define: What is income?

At first you might think that this is like defining what the word "is" is. Most businesses calculate income on either the cash or accrual basis of accounting. Believe it or not, once you make the election you need to get permission from the IRS to change. This one issue alone can make a big difference on whether you defer income or accelerate income for tax purposes.

Calculation of depreciation.
You can choose straight-line or MACRS, bonus or no bonus, take section 179 or choose not to take sections 179. Do you choose a short life or longer life depreciation?

Industry specific decisions.
Added to the mix of determinants, there will most likely be a list of decisions necessary to make based on your specific industry. For example, if you are a general contractor you can recognize income on the completed contract method or the percentage of completion method mixed with the cash vs. accrual basis.

> **Are you starting to see how business owners get confused and end up going down the wrong path?**

Combine this with the general population's fear of the IRS and you can see the need for a method or process to help navigate the taxation process. This is why I developed the **Kissling Tax Method™.**

Simply put, I developed this method as a tax-planning process with one task in mind: to assist clients in maximizing their wealth by reducing their federal, state and local tax liabilities on both a current and long-term basis.

Lifestyle Determination.
To take advantage of the tax saving tactics I have developed, you should start with a determination of your lifestyle. My job is to help you with your taxes, not to make decisions about how you spend your money. I have always been an advocate of the belief that if you earn your living, you also earn the right to spend your money as you wish. However, if you are going to take advantage of tax savings, we

have to establish a beginning point. It is necessary to determine your spending habits.

For example, if you make a $1,000,000 per year and spend $1,000,000 per year, you will not be able to take advantage of most of the **Kissling Tax Method™**. Let's remember that the basic premise of wealth building is to spend less than you earn.

A look at the legal structure.
Next, we need to take a look at the legal structure of your business. Many times I find that people are overpaying their taxes simply because the legal structure of their business has not been set up to their best advantage.

Many times I find that people are overpaying their taxes simply because the legal structure of their business has not been set up to their best advantage.

The most common structure I see is a subchapter S corporation ("S-Corp."). The advantage of an S-Corp. is that the earnings of the business pass through to the owners without being taxed at the corporation level. The disadvantage is that the earnings of the business pass through to the owners without being taxed at the corporation level. You read correctly; this is not an editing error. The reality is that when structuring a business, it is necessary to analyze the advantages and disadvantages, and to develop the structure that best meets the needs of the owner.

A real-life illustration.

Meet Fred, the owner of a toothpick manufacturing company that has been very successful over the last 10 years. I met Fred years after he had consulted with another CPA regarding the structure of his company. I find his story to be very educational.

In the beginning, Fred managed his business as a sole proprietorship. Because Fred operated in an industry with limited legal liability risk, he felt comfortable functioning without the legal protection of a corporation.

A few years ago, Fred complained to his CPA about all of the taxes he was paying. He asked if his CPA had any suggestions on how to save taxes (notice that Fred had to ask). After some thought, his CPA asked him to consider incorporating and electing to be an S-Corp.

Fred had been making about $600,000 per year. As a sole proprietor, he had been required to pay self-employment tax, which is Social Security and Medicare tax, on 100% of his business earnings. This tax was $27,519 each year.

By converting his business to an S-Corp., Fred would only be required to tax what the IRS defines as a "reasonable salary." A reasonable salary would be a salary similar to a typical salary of someone performing the same duties that Fred performs on a daily basis.

In Fred's case, it was determined that a "reasonable salary" would be $75,000 per year. The Social Security and Medicare tax on $75,000 is $11,475, *saving Fred over $16,000 every year. This made Fred very excited. What Fred hadn't yet figured out was that as exciting as it is to save $16,000, he had still not saved a dime of income tax.*

As a tax planner, I completely agree with Fred's CPA on the reasonable salary point. I have given this same advice over a 100 times. But it is essential that we not stop at the easy savings. We really need to look at the big picture.

The next year, Fred complained about the taxes he was paying. Fred had already forgotten about the $16,000 he was saving, because he was still paying the IRS over $170,000 in income taxes. Fred's CPA suggested initiating a retirement plan. He explained that by setting up a retirement plan, Fred could take a tax deduction today while he is in a high tax bracket for money he sets aside for retirement. The earnings would grow on a tax-deferred basis. Then, Fred could take the money out of his retirement plan later, when he expected to be in a lower tax bracket.

Once again Fred was excited. He would save more than half of his take-home money and get a tax deduction.

Of course Fred wanted to maximize his deduction, which is why he asked his CPA how to do that. The CPA suggested that Fred set up a safe harbor 401K plan. If he wanted to, Fred could put his wife on the *payroll in order to get a larger overall deduction. This set up Fred with a new salary of $150,000 for himself and $20,000 for his wife. (By having a larger salary for Fred he could get a larger company match to his contributions.) As a result of all this maneuvering, Fred seemed happy to save another $13,000 in taxes, for a total of almost $31,000 savings from his original situation.*

I am skeptical whether Fred has really saved any money at all. First of all, when Fred set up the 401K-retirement plan for himself, he had to set up

Before Fred's former CPA moved forward with his proposal, he should have taken the time to ask Fred a few useful questions:

- *What do you use your money for?*
- *What is your financial life style?*
- *Do you spend all of your money or do you save and invest a certain portion of your money?*
- *What will be your financial needs in the future?*
- *Are there any unusual, upcoming expenses?*
- *Do you need to maintain a certain level of working capital inside your company?*
- *What is the exit plan for your company?*
- *Will you be selling your company at a future date?*
- *Do you have children who will take over the company?*
- *What are the costs vs. the benefits of the program?*

*the same plan for his employees. This added $25,000
to his cost of operations. Fred's CPA at the time, like
many accountants and financial planners, forgot to
look at the big picture.*

*When we employ the **Kissling Tax Method**™, we
take the time to look at the entire legal structure.
Many business owners have not realized that there
are certain tax deductions allowed as a subchapter
C corporation that are not deductible under an
S-Corp. structure, for example. In my practice, we
take advantage of all the tax deductions we can by
setting up many of our clients as both an S-Corp. and
a C-Corp.*

Our job is to maximize cash flow and to build wealth. If for a
particular client that simply involves a traditional pension plan, that
is fine. But we need to look at all of the alternatives before moving
forward.

I cannot state this too often: my goal as a financial advisor is to serve
my clients by minimizing their tax liability and enabling their ability to
maximize their wealth to retain a high quality of life for retirement.
With this mission in mind, let us explore more real life examples of
tactics I have successfully employed to save money for clients.

Joe's Bookkeeper's Question.

Once, I was taken aback when a client's bookkeeper

asked me; "Shouldn't we have a retirement plan? Wouldn't it be in Joe's best interest to be saving money for his retirement? After all, I have a retirement plan at my part-time job and I only work there two days a week." It was an eye-opening conversation.

Joe had been a client of mine for over 10 years. Joe's company had already utilized some of the tactics that I employ in my practice. However, even though Joe's bookkeeper issued the checks resulting from the tactics, obviously she did not understand the underlying goals that Joe and I had outlined to plan his retirement.

My ultimate goal is to create wealth for my clients so that they do not need to employ traditional wealth-building methods that focus only on tax deferral, rather than tax elimination.

When the Kissling Tax Method™ is employed, the focus is on my client's wealth, not on my client's employees' wealth. Employees are important, and I do care about their welfare. However, my duty is to my client first and his employees second.

When the Kissling Tax Method™ is employed, the focus is on my client's wealth, not on my client's employees' wealth.

The bookkeeper was concerned about her own retirement plan, not her employer's. I had to explain to her that Joe already had a significant retirement plan and that the cost of setting up a 401K plan would outweigh the benefits he would derive from such a plan.

What we set up for Joe:

- *The big picture and realization of the value of his ongoing business.*
- *Roth IRA's.*
- *Closely Held Insurance Company.*
- *Non-qualified investments*
- *US Possession Companies that are profitable and will be available to support his retirement in the future.*

Joe's bookkeeper is a great bookkeeper. However, she is a "traditionalist." She believes that a retirement plan only comes in a form that is labeled by the IRS as a "retirement plan." I coined the phrase **Think Beyond Now™** *in an effort to get clients to think outside of the box with regard to taxes. I want clients to take themselves out of their current situations and to look at the world a little differently.*

───※───

I see my job as a wealth planner as an opportunity to help my clients build their financial assets to a level that will provide them the cash flow necessary to support their desired lifestyles in the later years of their lives.

We call financial vehicles many different things, but their purpose is always the same: to act as a tax-efficient retirement plan.

If you are interested in more particulars about the list of tactical items above, be patient. We will get more deeply into those alternative plans or tactics later.

In the meanwhile, *If your tax attorney or CPA isn't approaching your goals and needs this way, and isn't asking some of these same questions, you need to ask yourself, "Why?"*

> *"Success depends upon previous preparation, and without such preparation there is sure to be failure."* **Confucius**

Retirement Plans

The only reason to put money into a deferred tax program is when you can guarantee that you will be in a lower tax bracket in the future. **TK.**

As a business owner, you may have various reasons for associating a retirement plan with your company. You may use a tax-deferred vehicle to save for your own retirement, a tax-deferred vehicle to help your employees save for their retirement, or both.

Unfortunately, often the only reason a business owner sets up a retirement plan is because his CPA has advised that it is the only approach currently available for saving on taxes. As a CPA myself, I realize that this certification alone does not create the most proactive and aggressive financial planners.

The best guidance for business owners comes from a hybrid entrepreneur and CPA. Someone who possesses the kind of passion and ambition necessary to proactively guide clients to make the best financial decisions, or retirement planning decisions.

Regardless of your reasons in the past, it is beneficial to review how retirement plans actually work. Then you can make an educated decision to determine whether or not your current plan is in line with your goals.

Qualified vs. Non-qualified Retirement Plans.

In order for you to gain a basic understanding of the range of retirement plans, I will break down the various types and categories of plans. First let's look at "qualified" vs. "non-qualified."

Department of the Treasury
Internal Revenue Service

The term "qualified" indicates that the plan meets all of the IRS and Department of Labor required statutory and regulatory requirements to qualify as a tax-deductible expense.

A "non-qualified" plan obviously does not meet the statutory and regulatory requirements and is therefore not tax-deductable. But, as you will see later, non-qualified plans are still valid financial vehicles for saving taxes.

Two Categories of Qualified Plans.
Qualified plans can be further broken down into two categories: Defined Benefit or Defined Contribution.

Defined Benefit Plans are what I describe as a traditional pension plan.   For example, an employee goes to work for a company and the company makes annual contributions to the employee's pension fund. After serving a certain number of years and reaching a certain age, the employee can retire and be paid a certain monthly payment (a "defined benefit"), for the rest of his or her life. Put simply, the employer is providing a fund to allow the employee to receive a life annuity payout. These are the kind of plans with which Joe's bookkeeper would be familiar.

The Challenge is Actuarial.
The challenge to a company with Defined Benefit Plans is that each year the company must engage the services of an actuary to determine if it has contributed enough money to the pension to provide assurances that the pension fund will have sufficient funds to

meet the long-term pension payments that are guaranteed to its employees. An actuary gathers information about the company's employees related to the number of years of service, age, and gender.

Based upon this information, the actuary uses his expertise to calculate the amount that is needed in the pension fund to fund the company's future pension liabilities. After the future liability has been determined, the actuary will calculate the amount of money that needs to be placed into the pension fund to make sure the fund can meet its obligations based upon an assumed future average rate of return on the plan's investments.

Once the actuary has determined the amount of investment holdings the fund is required to hold, he will issue a report to inform the company of the amount of money that must be deposited into the pension plan to keep the plan in compliance. This amount will be the current year's contribution and the amount of the tax deduction to which the company will be entitled.

With this understanding of how a Defined Benefit Plan works, we can now take a look at some of the negative traits of a Defined Benefit Plan.

Your individual goals will determine whether any of the traits have a positive or negative impact on your company.

TRAIT #1: Administrative costs can be expensive.

You will have fees associated with the actuary, third party administrator, possibly auditor, and third party custodian. These costs are usually covered by the employer.

TRAIT #2: The annual actuarial study is subject to many assumptions.

Actuaries make assumptions related to the estimated rate of return on the plan's investments and the estimated mortality rate of the participants. Whenever you rely on assumptions you have a risk of error. There is a risk that an assumption may require a change that could increase the long-term pension liability. This change could result in an unexpected minimum required payment at an inopportune time.

TRAIT #3: Poor investment results could leave the plan underfunded.

If the plan's underlying investments underperform the actuaries' assumed rate of return, the plan's current balance could come up short. The employer is ultimately responsible for the shortfall.

If all of these traits seem negative, that is with good reason; they have been part of the downfall of many companies over the last 30 years. It is my belief that they will be the downfall of many state and local governments in the future. For these reasons, most companies with a large number of employees have moved away from this type of retirement plan because they tend to be expensive and risky.

However, there are certain circumstances in which a Defined Benefit Plan is a great method to save a lot of money for retirement, quickly and efficiently. To better understand a Defined Benefit Plan as a positive method for saving, let's take a look at Bill's pension plan.

Bill's Beneficial Pension Plan.

After years of struggling to build his company, Bill suddenly found himself in his late 50's with a very successful business. He had not saved for retirement, but is now earning about $1 million per year.

Bill's company has 10 employees, all of whom are young (average age of 26). Bill wants to save as much retirement money as possible in the next five years and then retire. So he set up a Defined Benefit Plan and hired an actuary to determine the amount he could legally have his company contribute to his pension. The result was that Bill could set aside approximately $400,000 in the first year.

The contribution has to be allocated to each of the participants based upon the retirement criteria as dictated by the pension plan. Since Bill is close to retirement and has been employed by his company for a long time, and the other employees are young and a long way away from retirement, 95% of the contribution was allocated to Bill's account.

If Bill can maintain his current income levels, he will be able to contribute over $1 million to the plan over the next five years with the vast majority being allocated to Bill's personal benefit.

Defined Contribution Plans.
Where a Defined Benefit Plan focuses on future retirement benefits, a Defined Contribution Plan focuses on how much will be currently contributed to a plan without concern for the future benefits paid to employees. Where Defined Benefit Plans tend to focus on a group fund as a whole, a Defined Contribution Plan focuses on individual account balances of each employee.

Defined Contribution Plans have become more popular than Defined Benefit Plans with employers over the last 30 years. Defined Contribution Plans tend to be less costly to operate and, more importantly, they shift the legal responsibility for making sure retirees have sufficient funds to retire, from the employer to the employee. If an employee fails to set aside enough money in a Defined Contribution Plan to properly retire, or if the retirement investments do not perform adequately, the shortfall is the employee's problem. The reverse is true with a Defined Benefit Plan, where the employer would be liable for any financial shortfalls.

Defined Contribution Plans include:
- SEP's
- Simple IRA's
- 401K Plans
- 403B Plans

The above chart reflects many of the Defined Contribution Plans available to employers. The list is fairly exhausting. Once again, the plan most appropriate for your company depends on your specific set of circumstances.

401K Plans.
401K plans are the most popular and well-known Defined Contribution Plan. For this reason, we will take a little time exploring them. 401K plans can also be referred to as Employee Savings Plans, Thrift Savings Plans and several other names. It has been my experience that the 401K is the easiest financial tool available to save money for retirement on a tax-deferred basis. Most people like the fact that a small amount of money is taken out of their paycheck each week. Because it is a small amount, most people do not even notice the reduction in their net paycheck. They are also popular because most employers match the amount that the employees have withheld at some percentage level.

Pros and cons of 401K Plan for the Business Owner.
The concept of a 401K is very good from an employee's perspective. From an employer's perspective it depends on your specific situation. If you have more than 100 employees and you do not want to incur the costs of a Defined Benefit Plan, a 401K plan may be your best choice.

Within the array of choices available for Defined Contribution Plans, most of them do not make sense once a company has more than 100 employees.

If a company has less than 100 employees, there are more economic methods, such as the SIMPLE-IRA, that will help employees accomplish their retirement savings goals with less administrative fees.

If you have a 401K plan at your company, I suggest that you take a good look at the administrative fees associated with your plan.

My experience is that there are a lot of hidden fees with most plans. Beware of plans from insurance companies.

When it comes to retirement plans, business owners have been convinced to maximize their contributions to their company's 401K plan to help save taxes.

It is a fact that I have "fired" many spouses throughout my career.

I have seen owners put their spouses on the payroll just so the spouse could contribute to the 401K. For the most part, I view this practice to be foolish and impractical. It is a fact that I have "fired" many spouses throughout my career.

An example of why I've fired many spouses during my career.

Remember my client, Fred? When Fred first came to me, he had already put his wife on the payroll with an annual salary of $20,000 so that she could contribute $15,000 to the company 401K.

Fred (as well as his former CPA) had not thought through the cost of having his spouse on the payroll.

By putting his wife on the payroll, Fred had to pay 15.3% in social security and Medicare taxes. He had to cover federal and state unemployment taxes. And, finally, he had to cover workers' compensation.

At the end of the day, it is fair to assume that it cost 20% of wages, or $4,000, to take a $15,000 tax deduction. The $4,000 cost is actually 26.67% of the $15,000 contributed to the 401K. I'm sure Fred considered the fact that they are in a 40% tax bracket. $15,000 x 40% is a $6,000 tax savings. Therefore, the net savings is $2,000.

Unfortunately, Fred missed the greatest issue. He will be in a 40% tax bracket in the future. Fred paid $4,000 and will give more than that back when he and his wife draw out the retirement money in the future.

Needless to say, I advised Fred that he needed to fire his spouse. Both husband and wife were in agreement on that decision!

Individual Retirement Accounts (IRAs).
The majority of the business owners who take advantage of the **Kissling Tax Method™** will not be making contributions to IRA accounts. Because, as they become more successful and earn more money, the government thinks that it would be unfair for them to take advantage of this small tax deferral.

Given that I am not a big fan of tax deferral for reasons I will discuss later in Chapter 5 this may be a blessing in disguise.

Under current IRS regulations, if you are married and have an adjusted gross income over $115,000, you cannot contribute to a traditional IRA account.

However, for most people, you will have an IRA at some point and you

should know how it works so that you can make wise decisions when it is appropriate.

IRA accounts were introduced in the early 1980's, and at the time they seemed like a great deal. This particular form of Defined Contribution Plan was set up to allow individuals to defer taxes at a high tax bracket until retirement when they would likely be in a low tax bracket. In the early 1980's this was all true. It was a great deal: take a deduction at 50% and pay it back later at 30%. It seemed the tax payer was winning the battle for once.

My own personal IRA reminiscence.

I remember preparing my parents' tax returns back when I was 20-year-old college student. I could see that my parents were in a 50% marginal tax bracket (in the early 1980's a taxpayer could earn less than $50,000 per year and be in a 50% tax bracket.)
So, in order to save taxes, my parents contributed $2,000 to an IRA, which was the maximum allowable contribution at the time, and received a $1,000 savings on their taxes. It seemed like a great deal. Frankly, it was.

That $2,000 grew at 6% per year for the next 30 years. By then, my parents were in a 15% tax bracket.

The fund grew to $11,500. After paying taxes of $1,725 they ended up with an after tax amount of $9,775 from an after-tax investment of $1,000. My parents walked away with almost 10 times their initial investment after 30 years.

———— ⊗≋⊗ ————

This growth experience is exactly what hooked everyone into IRA accounts.

However, the problem with having IRA accounts is the substantial change in the income tax code in 1986. When the federal government was finished revamping the tax code, the country ended up with a tax code that eliminated many tax deductions in exchange for lowering the marginal tax brackets.

Consequently, we do not have 50% tax brackets any more. Now most people are in the 15% tax bracket, or possibly the 25% bracket. So there is a limited ability to defer into a lower tax bracket.

The only reason to put money into a deferred tax program is when you can guarantee that you will be in a lower tax bracket in the future. If you are a successful businessperson, you will likely be limited in this ability.

Despite the fact that I am not a big fan of making contributions to IRA accounts, the reality is that most people have already headed down the path of having an IRA. So, it is important to know how the rules work. If you are participating in a Defined Benefit or Defined Contribution Plan, you will at some time want to move your money out of those plans. The only way to transfer those funds to another investment vehicle and to continue to defer the taxes on those funds is to transfer them (or rollover) to an IRA account. That is one reason I say there is a pretty good chance that you will have an IRA at some time.

The most important rule to observe regarding IRS's is to not plan on taking your funds from your IRA prior to age 59 ½. Generally, distributions prior to that age are subject to regular income taxes at your current tax bracket, plus an additional 10% tax penalty.

I can't tell you how many times I have advised clients that taking money out of their IRA before age 59 ½ is a bad financial move. By the time you pay your taxes and the penalty, the average taxpayer will lose about 1/3 of the amount taken out.

If you are a successful businessperson, it could very easily be 50%.
If this is the case, I think that, all things considered, it would be a smarter financial move to simply borrow the money from a bank.

There are exceptions to the penalty rules, such as using the funds to pay for higher education or certain medical expenses.

> *I can't tell you how many times I have advised clients that taking money out of their IRA before age 59 1/2 is a bad financial move.*

Further, if you take the funds out over a 5-year period, you can also avoid the 10% penalty, but you will never avoid paying the taxes.

If, for example, you retire prior to age 59½, you could consider taking a distribution from your IRA over a 5-year period to avoid the 10% penalty. This is referred to as rule 72t. I highly recommend you work with your CPA and financial advisor to make sure you follow all of the rules and regulations. A simple error could be expensive.

The second most important rule is that you must start taking money out of your IRA (or any other qualified retirement account) starting at age 70 ½. The amount that you need to take out of your IRA is generally referred to as your "Required Minimum Distribution" or RMD.

The RMD calculation is actually a very simple calculation. Take your total IRA and Defined Contribution account balances on January 1 each year and divide by the age factor found on the chart provided by the IRS.

Age	Distribution Period	Age	Distribution Period	Age	Distribution Period	Age	Distribution Period
70	27.4	82	17.1	94	9.1	106	4.2
71	26.5	83	16.3	95	8.6	107	3.9
72	25.6	84	15.5	96	8.1	108	3.7
73	24.7	85	14.8	97	7.6	109	3.4
74	23.8	86	14.1	98	7.1	110	3.1
75	22.9	87	13.4	99	6.7	111	2.9
76	22.0	88	12.7	100	6.3	112	2.6
77	21.2	89	12.0	101	5.9	113	2.4
78	20.3	90	11.4	102	5.5	114	2.1
79	19.5	91	10.8	103	5.2	115 and over	1.9
80	18.7	92	10.2	104	4.9		
81	17.9	93	9.6	105	4.5		

It is very important not to miss this distribution. The penalty for missing the distribution is 50% of the RMD that you missed. A simple "I forgot" can be very expensive.

Typically, most business owners who come to me already have IRA's. It becomes my challenge to manage the IRA's from a tax efficiency perspective. For the most part, if I am advising a business owner with an IRA, I will recommend: stop contributing to the IRA in favor of a more tax-efficient financial vehicle.

These alternatives are either a Roth or a Non-Qualified retirement account, depending on the client's situation. I will also focus on the best time to start liquidating the IRA.

Typically, most business owners who come to me already have IRAs and so it becomes my challenge to manage them from a tax efficiency perspective.

Roth's.

If we go back to the basic premise that the key to building wealth is spending less money than you earn, then it follows that you need to have tax efficient methods to grow those funds.

The Roth is a good savings vehicle if you qualify. In fact, I may go as far as saying that everyone that qualifies should have one of these. You can set aside $6,000 per year. The contribution to a Roth account is not tax deductable. However, as long as you hold a Roth for at least five years and wait until age 59 ½ before taking the funds out, the growth is 100% tax-free.

Further, if you find that you never need these funds, you can pass the account to your children or grandchildren upon your death, and they can let the funds grow tax-free for their entire lives.

A closer look at the Roth.

First of all, if your Adjusted Gross Income (AGI) is greater than $188,000 ($127,000 if you are single) then you cannot contribute to a Roth. Once again, the government has decided that the benefits of this particular financial vehicle are so good that the "rich" should not be allowed to participate.

I usually suggest countering with a couple of legal moves that would help my clients reduce their AGI below this level. If this isn't possible, I typically look at the process of contributing to a non-deductible IRA and immediately converting the IRA to a Roth.

The process takes a little paperwork, but it is both legal and effective.

Another way to contribute to a Roth if you have income over the limitation is to make a Roth contribution to your 401K.

Just a few years ago, the laws related to Defined Contribution Plans were changed to allow for Roth contributions. This means that employee contributions to a 401K plan or 403B plan would be treated like a Roth contribution.

The contributions are not tax-deductible, but the earnings on those contributions will not be taxed in the future. When you retire or change jobs you can transfer your Roth contributions to a Roth IRA rather than a traditional IRA.

If you are a business owner, I will more often than not recommend that you avoid the traditional retirement accounts. That is because they focus too much on tax deferral, which I do not see as very beneficial in the long run. This is because most of my business owner clients never move to a lower tax bracket in the future.

Let's take a moment to talk about tax-deferral. It sounds great. However, my personal experience is that many people are deferring at a low tax bracket and being forced to pay taxes at a higher tax bracket in the future. We will continue this subject in Chapter 5.

I work with business owners to focus on either tax-deductible today and tax-free upon retirement, or partially tax-deductable today and tax-free upon retirement.

If you think about it, most retirement plans are tax-deductable today and taxable upon retirement. That means that the taxes are simply deferred to the future. I want to eliminate as many taxes as legally possible.

> *The **Kissling Tax Method™** combines the best of both methods: tax-deductable AND tax-free income.*
>
> *And yes, it is legal!*

If you take the Roth option, you are trading a current tax deduction for a tax-free benefit later.

The **Kissling Tax Method™** combines the best of both methods: tax-deductable AND tax-free income.

And yes, it is legal!

Non-qualified retirement plans.

The non-qualified retirement plan has been around for several years, but is employed by relatively few CPA's.

Traditionally, non-qualified retirement plans are set up to help key employees defer a certain portion of their compensation until some future date. It is meant to be a benefit for employees, but has limited short-term benefit to employers. However, when you are both the employer and employee, you can work the plan to your benefit.

The plan involves setting up a special legal entity as a management or marketing company. Further, it involves properly writing and documenting a compensation plan for the new entity's management, which happens to be the business owner.

In the right circumstances, and with the proper legal structure, a business owner can take advantage of the lower tax brackets of a C corporation during his working years and convert the deferred compensation to a tax-free retirement account in the future.

Remember, the key to successfully building a retirement fund large enough to support yourself for a long retirement is to start early. My experience has been that most of my clients with substantial retirement account balances got there through methodically saving over a long period of time.

Remember this maxim, as well: the power of compounded interest is greatest over a long period of time. Those who start saving at age 35 have to put a lot more money away each month than those who start at age 20, in order to reach the same desired results upon retirement.

If your tax attorney or CPA isn't approaching your goals and needs this way, and isn't asking some of these same questions, you need to ask yourself, "Why?"

> *"1913 wasn't a very good year. 1913 gave us the income tax, the 16th amendment and the IRS."* **Ron Paul**

The Drawbacks of Tax Deferral Retirement Planning

Most people who plan to retire at age 65 do not think beyond that milestone. If you **Think Beyond Now™**, you soon realize that intelligent planning has to be made for all retirement years, not just reaching the milestone of age 65. **TK.**

We are most often told by financial advisors and CPA's that the most efficient way to build wealth is to defer income taxes whenever possible. Why pay a tax today that you can put off until tomorrow? The concept of *tax deferral* has been most prominent in the retirement planning world.

The problem with this concept is that it is a concept for the moment. It doesn't involve looking around the bend in that road I previously described to you. It doesn't involve a **Think Beyond Now™** perspective. In fact, when I was new to the accounting profession after graduating from college, I was literally taught to do whatever possible to save taxes in the current year and worry about the future in the future.

A Tax-deferral Retrospective.
When IRA's and 401K's were first introduced, the concept of *tax deferral* made sense. The basic concept was that the taxpayer could take a tax deduction today at a high tax rate and pull the funds out of his IRS/401K upon retirement when he would be in a lower tax bracket.

This was a great concept in 1980 when marginal tax rates were high. It's not as useful now when marginal tax rates are considerably lower.

Here are some examples of *tax deferral* that serve as good arguments against using this as your main means of retirement planning.

Let's say that 30 years ago you had the discipline and foresight to set aside $5,000 per year until you retire.

Remember my client Joe?

> When I first met Joe, a new tax client, he had already determined to do that very thing.
>
> The way Joe figured, if he simply deferred the tax on his account over 30 years, he would retire with an account balance of approximately $396,000. (Just a quick side note – you should quickly see that you need to save much more than $5,000 per year to set up an adequate retirement account.)

> *But the fact is, he paid the taxes on the non-deferred account. The tax-deferred account still has a liability of $158,000 at a 40% tax rate.*

In a parallel scenario, had Joe taken the same $5,000 and invested in a traditional, non-qualified account, and paid taxes at a rate of 40% per year, his account balance would have been approximately $262,000. The tax-deferred account would be 50% higher than the non-deferred account.

In comparing these two scenarios, Joe felt better about his retirement account being $396,000 than the theoretical $262,000 in the non-deferred account. But the fact is, he would have already paid the taxes on the non-deferred account. The tax-deferred account still has a liability of $158,000 at a 40% tax rate. By the time the tax liability is subtracted from the deferred account balance, he would have less money than the non-deferred account ($396,000-$158,000 = $238,000).

You might challenge this assertion by arguing that Joe would be in a lower tax bracket when he retires. That's assuming that Joe would be paying income taxes less than a 40% tax rate in retirement.

The trouble with this assumption is that Joe, like so many of my business owner clients, has acquired the habit of earning money. It is in his make-up to make money. And the habit isn't something

> *My clients tend to be successful business people who have acquired a habit of making good money. They plan to retire with more money than they need.*

that changes suddenly.

The truth is, most of my clients are successful business people who have acquired a habit of making good money. They plan to retire with more money than they need. Therefore, they are more likely than not to be in at least as high a tax bracket upon retirement as they have been during their working years. That is certainly the case with Joe.

Another revealing glimpse of tax reality. At the time of my writing this book, we experienced a significant tax rate increase on taxpayers who earn more than $200,000 per year and $400,000 per year in the United States.

Single taxpayers with unearned income and taxable income over $200,000 per year just got hit with a 3.8% Medicare tax.

For single taxpayers with taxable incomes over $400,000, Congress created a new 39.8% tax bracket (up from 35%).

So now, high net-worth taxpayers have been slapped with a potential 8.6% tax increase.

Do you really anticipate tax rates will be lower in the future when you retire? Of course not!

Sometimes, through no fault of our own, but through faulty planning by others, we find ourselves in a higher income level slapped with considerable penalties.

Mary's inheritance conundrum.
Mary and her husband Chad just inherited a significant amount of money from Mary's parents. When Mary came to see me she had many questions about the deferred annuities that she was inheriting.

The annuities had grown from $300,000 to $500,000 over several years. Because the earnings inside an annuity are tax-deferred, Mary and Chad will need to pay tax on the $200,000 gain that Mary's parents had deferred. Mary was concerned about the income taxes because they are already in a higher tax bracket. In fact, they are in the 33% federal tax bracket.

Here is another case where tax-deferment does no favors for the heirs of the well-intentioned parents. Mary's parents thought they were doing their children a great service by saving their money on a tax-deferred basis. Unfortunately, the reality is that Mary and Chad will be faced with a tax bill in the 33% to 35% range.

The parents were in a 15% tax bracket. They deferred income tax at 15% and now their kids are paying tax at 35%. I can tell you that my client, Mary, is not a fan of tax deferral.

These stories of tax deferral illustrate the tragic mistakes commonly made by many who actually have been advised to do this by their own well-intentioned financial advisors, tax attorneys or CPA's.

As a business owner, you have probably received many invitations to seminars, dinners and lectures on retirement planning and tax deferment. I know that as a businessperson myself, I have!

The main focus of most of these advisors is traditional retirement planning. Not a lot has changed for them over the years. I am here to tell you that if you are serious about paying less in taxes now, and in your retirement, you have to become proactive, thinking outside the box. It's part of my **Think Beyond Now™** strategy.

This is the message I share with audiences when I conduct seminars across the country. It's funny that though it may be the first time someone has revealed these secrets to them, it always rings true with my affluent audience members!

Consider the personality profile of most people who are successful in saving money and building wealth. Almost always, people who are adept at saving money during their working years also are good at not spending their money in retirement.

> *Almost always, people who are adept at saving money during their working years also are good at not spending their money in retirement.*

That is one reason why I find that, more often than not, individuals with large IRA accounts do not really need them for retirement.

Typically, having continued beyond retirement to live their lives in the frugal manner to which they had become accustomed, they leave a large tax-deferred account to their children. Their children then end up paying higher taxes when they inherit the tax-deferred accounts.

Sadly this is all too common among well-meaning parents who have attempted to live responsibly with their earnings and wealth.

Keeping in mind that tax-deferment used as the only implement for retirement planning can be a detriment to yourself as well as your heirs, it is imperative you begin immediately to look at more effective ways in to plan for your own retirement.

If your tax attorney or CPA isn't approaching your goals and needs this way, and isn't asking some of these same questions, you need to ask yourself, "Why?"

The other side of retirement.
Saving for retirement is one of our primary responsibilities during our working years. But have you looked at the tax picture on the other side of retirement? Do you understand the difference between tax deferral and tax free? Has your financial advisor or CPA explained this to you?

When you start to closely inspect the benefits and the restrictions of your retirement plan, typical of most business owners, you will realize that in order to best benefit from your existing plan, you need to plan to live to age 100. The bottom line is that we are living longer. Thus, we need to save more money to cover more retirement years.

Most people who plan to retire at age 65 do not think beyond that milestone. If you **Think Beyond Now™**, you soon realize that intelligent planning has to be made for all retirement years, not just reaching the milestone of age 65. Tax planning does not stop upon retirement. The truth is, when you do the math, you will realize your retirement years could be 35+ years.

We have been taught to take advantage of tax-deferred savings plans such as 401K's and IRA's because they save us taxes now. You most likely deferred taxes while in your working years, during which you had more deductions and dependents.

While you were busy building a business, you probably acquired debt in the process. At the same time, you have probably bought a house and are now raising children. Are they attending college?

As overwhelming as your current responsibilities may be, eventually, the tax deductions related to these responsibilities will phase out. When you successfully pay off your mortgage and many of your early business loans or when your youngest child graduates from college, the sense of elation in your newfound freedom may be short-lived, because you don't have as many tax deductions.

Retirement is on the horizon, and you will most likely find yourself in a much higher tax bracket than you expected. And, this does not even consider the question of whether the federal government will raise tax rates in the future.

What will happen when the time comes for you to retire and tap your 401K? How will your 401K plan serve you then? What percentage of taxes will you or your loved ones pay on the distribution from your 401K savings from state and federal taxes?

> *Because we haven't reached that age of retirement, we don't foresee the unknown crisis that awaits us around that bend.*

Remember to Think Beyond Now™. It is quite common among hard-working business owners: we postpone the reality of paying taxes hoping that the day never comes. We are so busy earning a living and building our businesses that we don't stop to plan ahead.

Because we haven't reached that age of retirement, we don't foresee the unknown crisis that awaits us around that bend. My road analogy reminds us to be prepared for all of those unforeseen circumstances, or curves in the road. We need to become proactive rather than always reacting to bumps in the road with quick fixes.

More than one of my clients has learned and benefited from this lesson. With our guidance, they have managed to retool their retirement plans to accommodate some of these more proactive tactics of the **Kissling Tax Method™**.

"Someday" comes fast, and when we look back to all those bumps in the road, we don't want to regret not having had the foresight to plan for those eventualities, and for the retirement years.

Just like the federal government ignoring its staggering debt until the crisis is undeniable, we continue along our path not taking the time to ensure that our retirement plan is truly leading to better wealth and prosperity.

> *We are saving for a future day, but it's a day that has a huge pay-off for Uncle Sam, too.*

We are saving for a future day, but it's a day that has a huge pay-off for Uncle Sam, too.

Now you may be beginning to understand why the federal government is so willing to allow you to defer taxes on your 401K plan. Your tax deferral is a bonanza for Uncle Sam in your retirement years.

Getting a higher altitude perspective on retirement while you are still working is crucial for your wellbeing in your retirement years. One of my main goals, professionally, is to legally save as many tax dollars in the working years and pay as little tax as possible in the retirement years.

Traditional planners focus on tax deferral and hope and pray things work out in the future. The **Kissling Tax Method**™ has a primary goal of saving tax dollars currently and during retirement.. We will talk about this in more detail in the following chapter.

I have many clients who have learned through their professional relationship with my practice, how to focus more and more on tax-free retirement. Deferral becomes less and less acceptable to them the more they have been educated on the subject.

I may have instilled sufficient fear in you to get your attention, but this book is not meant to be about gloom and doom. There really is hope for everyone to have a life that is more productive, and to enjoy a high-quality lifestyle in retirement.

A summary of the differences in retirement planning methods:

Traditional
Tax Deductions NOW
Taxable LATER
CPA's typically do this for their clients.
In the past this was "good enough."

Traditional "Tax-Free" Retirement
No Tax Deduction TODAY
Tax-Free at RETIREMENT
A more advanced tactic used in the
insurance industry. It's a "better"
method.

Kissling Tax Method™
Tax Deductible NOW
Tax Free at RETIREMENT
This is our goal whenever we can
possibly achieve it for our clients.
*It's the **best** method for a tax-free*
retirement.

Tax-Free Retirement.
How is tax-free retirement possible, you ask? I will answer that question with many examples in the next chapter as we take a look at some of the tools available for a tax-free retirement.

> *"Elections should be held on April 16th - the day after we pay our income taxes. That is one of the few things that might discourage politicians from being big spenders."* **Thomas Sowell**

Tax Savings via
the Kissling Tax Method™

The rules are set by both the IRS and by local insurance regulators. If you qualify and follow the rules properly, the tax benefits can be substantial. **TK.**

Take a serious look at your future tax brackets. Ask yourself: "Will I be in a higher tax bracket or a lower tax bracket in the future?"

Before you get to the point of no return, it is imperative to start considering the following questions now.

Will you, as a business owner, need a formal retirement plan? If it is truly a retirement plan, shouldn't your focus be on what might be anticipated to be the tax and economic climate when you retire?

But, you say, "I need tax deductions today." The question then becomes: "Am I better off paying some tax today in exchange for never paying taxes in the future?"

This is a good place to share with you some of the various tactics employed in the Kissling Tax Method™.

The question then becomes: "Am I better-off paying some tax today in exchange for never paying taxes in the future?"

It seems that whenever someone takes a step outside the box, society pushes back. Usually out of ignorance or arrogance. Trust me, I have been guilty of both, many times. It is often not to the benefit of the individual.

The formalization of the **Kissling Tax Method™** was the result of a process. I realized that I didn't know all that I needed to know in order to completely eliminate my clients' tax liabilities.

So I went on a mission. I knew there had to be portions of the tax code that were not being used to the best advantage of my clients. My search resulted in me connecting with a group of tax attorneys. We have worked together to develop an array of tactics that are benefiting my clients in substantial ways.

Once my clients see my ideas and the supporting documentation, they are amazed by the resulting potential changes to their tax liability.

Full disclosure: documentation.
Before I proceed further, there is one necessary disclosure I want to share. In this chapter, I will be explaining several methods that we use. Remember, with each method there is required documentation.

Many people lose the opportunity for tax deductions because they are too lazy to take the steps necessary to secure the tax deduction. If you are serious about living a tax-free retirement, you need to be serious about taking responsibility for your documentation as well.

*...the purpose of this book is to provoke you, the reader, to inquire for yourself if the **Kissling Tax Method™** might be a process worth exploring through a financial advisor.*

I am not going to elaborate upon each and every one of the tactics available to clients. Following is just a small sampling. The **Kissling Tax Method™** employs many more processes than what are being presented here.

The purpose of this book is to provoke you, the reader, to inquire for yourself if the **Kissling Tax Method™** might be a process worth exploring.

TACTIC #1: Meal Reimbursement Plan.
It is relatively well-known among business owners that business meals and entertainment are 50% deductible for federal income tax purposes. I hope these entrepreneurs also understand that a business purpose is necessary in order for the meal to be deductible and that the purpose must be documented.

It is, however, much less known that if your company has set up a properly documented meal reimbursement plan, you can reimburse employees for meals without even going to dinner. Let me give you an example.

Another real life example from my life.

Years ago, I worked for a CPA firm in Pittsburgh, Pennsylvania. My employer's company policy allowed all employees who worked more than 10 hours in one day to charge a $25 dinner to the company.

The meal was considered a fringe benefit. Meaning, the $25 dinner expense was an employee benefit that was tax deductible to my employer, not to me, the employee. The reason is because it was considered a meal for the convenience of the employer. My employer was willing to give me a meal so that I would stay at work longer and get my work done.

My employer concluded that it would be less efficient for me to leave the office for dinner, because I might not come back to complete my work.

The beautiful thing is that the IRS has allowed the meal deduction for many years. So there is no realistic chance that this would be challenged.

What is even better, is the fact that since this is for the convenience of the employer, the meal is 100% deductible rather than 50% deductible.

If I help you start a business entity with only the owners as employees, could we not set up a meal reimbursement plan that would allow owners to be reimbursed a couple of days a week for working overtime?

If we set up a plan for a company with a husband and wife as the owners that would reimburse each employee that worked more than 8.5 hours per day at the rate of $75 per day, could the result be $15,000 per year in tax-deductable expenses for the company and tax-free for them?

The answer is "Yes!" The question is: why aren't you doing this?

The above example alone adds up to nearly a $5,000 per year savings in taxes. You don't actually have to go out to dinner. You simply are required to complete an expense report and document your work hours. By the way, you really do need to work the hours. You can't just make them up.

On many occasions, I have discussed this tactic with my clients, only to find out that they **never** work overtime. This tactic does not apply to them. It is a substantial savings that is often missed by CPA's, so I make a point to always ask. Is your CPA asking?

I find that I need to leave my office a few times a year to be able to concentrate on the business of my business.

If you have missed the meal deduction for 10 years, you have potentially overpaid your taxes by $50,000.

TACTIC #2: Tax-Free Rental of Your Home or Vacation Home.
Did you know that there is a provision in the Internal Revenue code that would allow you to rent the use of your home for up to 14 days every year, tax-free? Did you know this provision has been around since the Eisenhower administration?

Many of my clients have vacation homes. They like to relax on the beach and enjoy the benefits of vacation. I need to ask you, the business owner, do you really ever completely go on vacation? I know that I don't.

I am actually sitting at a beach resort as I am writing this chapter of the book. I find that I need to leave my office a few times a year to be able to concentrate on the business of my business. I know that I am not the exception to the rule.

———— ❈ ————

Client benefit case in point.
I have a friend, Mike, who loves his cabin in the mountains. It is a luxury log home on a lake. Mike and his wife love being there and would like to live there. He goes there as often as he can.

When Mike, who is a business owner, goes to his cabin for a weekend, he tries to leave home a day early. The purpose of that extra day is to take a business day.

Instead of sitting in his office, he sits on the deck of his vacation home with his wife, going over the various business matters that they have difficulty addressing while in their normal work environment.

Many times, Mike and his wife bring business associates to their cabin for business conferences. Friday is business, and the rest of the weekend is personal fun time.

In this way, Mike's business rents the cabin from him one Friday per month so that he and his wife can have a business meeting. The fair market rental value of the property is $3,500 per day. Twelve days per year of rental activity is valued at $42,000 per year. This is a tax deduction to his corporation and it is tax-free to him.

In a 43% tax bracket, this is an annual tax savings of over $18,000!

My Own Home Plans.

I am planning to build a new house for myself. It has been my dream to build a house on a lake near my office.

Here's the amazing thing: this tax savings would actually pay most of my mortgage payment!

Rather than travel to my vacation home, I have decided that I want to live at my vacation home. As I am planning the house, I have been thinking about how I can rent this new property for no more than 14 days per year. How can I get a rebate for using my house for business purposes?

Some of my brainstorm ideas have included the following: the house could be rented out for wedding receptions. The media room could be designed to accommodate training classes for my staff and other financial professionals with whom I work. There are other options as well.

As long as I don't exceed 14 days of rental, it is tax-free. And here's the amazing thing: this tax savings would actually pay most of my mortgage payment! As you can see, the 14-days-of-rental-income tactic can be applied to any piece of real estate. Furthermore, you can take advantage of it for more than one piece of real estate at a time.

My friend, Mike, with the luxury log home, could also rent his personal residence. For those of you with more than one vacation home, you can rent them all out for 14 days, each, annually.

Before we move on to the next tactic you need to understand that 14 days is the hard limit. If you rent your home for a 15th day, you will be required to report the rental income as taxable from day one. It is retroactive.

TACTIC #3: Corporate Structure.
I have a client, whom I'll call Tony, who is a general contractor. Tony has significant amounts of equipment on the road and on construction sites on any given day. He has 75 employees working all over his state. Tony worries that someday he is going to get one of those calls no business owner wants to receive:

*The first company is simply a **holding company** that is the owner of three subsidiaries.*

An employee has driven one of Tony's trucks into a school bus and Tony does not have enough insurance to cover the liability. Or maybe a call about a piece of equipment that got away from an employee and caused more damage to someone's property than Tony's insurance covers.

So, Tony came to me and asked me how to restructure his company to further protect himself.

*Initially we focused on legal liability. Whether or not my client had to pay more in income taxes was not a priority at that point. So, we divided Tony's company into four pieces. The first company is simply a **holding company** that is the owner of three subsidiaries.*

*Subsidiary No. 1 is the **operating company.** This company enters into contracts with customers and buys materials from suppliers.*

*Subsidiary No. 2 is an **employment agency.** All of the employees work for this company and the operating company pays a fee for use of the employees.*

*Subsidiary No. 3 is an **equipment leasing company.** This company holds all of the construction company's equipment. The operating company pays an equipment usage fee to use the equipment leasing company's equipment.*

Tony's company now files a consolidated tax return so there is no real income tax affect as a result of this reorganization.

The reorganization was merely an effort to separate assets in the event of legal problems.

*After reviewing Tony's situation, I started to wonder if we could utilize the **Kissling Tax Method™**, in an effort to save Tony some income taxes.*

What if This Could Work for You?

There are specific operations performed by the operating company that could be outsourced to another company. Companies outsource work all the time. For example, many outsource the payroll process to an outside company.

When you need the expertise of a chief financial officer, you hire your CPA as a consultant. When you have personnel issues, you hire an outside consultant or attorney to assist you. So, what if you created a related company to handle all of these administrative issues?

What if you created an "outsource company" and kept all of the profits generated rather than give them to some unrelated company?

If we created an "Outsource Corporation," the sole purpose of the company would be to handle all of the administrative tasks that you normally outsource.

You could pay a monthly fee to the operating company and then when you needed the services, you could hire the outside company to provide the services.

If you didn't need the services this month, or this year, you could keep the profits in the Outsource Corporation. In this way, you have a tax deduction for the operating company and taxable income in the Outsource Corporation.

At this point, you might be asking yourself, "What have we created?" To review our actions, we shifted profits from Company A to Company B, so therefore you still have the same net income. However, employing the **Kissling Tax Method™** we domiciled the Outsource Corporation in an economically advantaged tax zone.

This concept is common among large corporations. Small business owners have this resource available to them, as well. However, most small business owners do not know how to build the multiple entity structure.

Consider the Apple Example.
Think about Apple Computer. All of their manufacturing is done in Asia.

Do you really think that they give all of the profits to the Asian manufacturers or do you think that maybe they have their own subsidiary company that acts as a middleman in Asia?

The taxable profits in Asia are held in a country with a substantially lower tax rate than in the United States.

The following is an interesting story about Apple that ran in *USA Today* in May of 2013.

"The California-based firm has used a web of offshore entities— including three Ireland subsidiaries that it said don't have tax residency in any country—to cut some of its tax rates to 0.05%, the Senate Permanent Subcommittee on Investigations reported.

"One of those Apple subsidiaries reported $30 billion in net income for 2009-2012, yet filed no corporate tax return and paid no income taxes to any government during those years, the panel reported in advance of a public hearing set for Tuesday.

"Another affiliate received $74 billion in sales income over four years, but paid taxes "on only a tiny fraction of that income," the report said.

"Apple also transferred economic rights for some of its intellectual property to its offshore affiliates in low-tax jurisdictions, saving tens of billions of dollars in levies, the Senate panel concluded in its latest look at corporate tax avoidance tactics."

USA Today, May 2013

We actually have the ability to do this income-shifting legally, within the borders of the United States. The federal government has created special economic zones where tax rates are lower than the normal federal income tax rates as an incentive to create jobs within those zones. Thus, we can domicile an outsource company in an economic zone that has a tax rate as low as 4%.

Large corporations use these tactics all the time, and there is no reason you, too, should not consider taking advantage of the same methods.

You have heard how large corporations have low, effective tax rates.

Income shifting is one of the methods employed to achieve the low rate. Large corporations use different tactics all the time, and there is no reason you, too, should not consider taking advantage of the same methods.

According to an article in the Wall Street Journal in January 2013, Google, Inc., Microsoft Corporation, and data-storage specialist EMC Corp., "keep more than three quarters of the cash owned by their foreign subsidiaries at U.S. banks, held in U.S. dollars or parked in U.S. government and corporate securities . . . as long as it doesn't flow back to the U.S. parent company, the U.S. doesn't tax it.

In that article, the author mentions that 67% of Apple's $110 billion total cash is foreign cash. Of Microsoft's $59.5 billion, 89% is foreign, and of Wal-Mart's $6.6 billion, 85% is foreign. The author explained that "Cash that companies permanently invest overseas isn't taxed

Profit Burden

Bristol-Myers estimates its tax rate will drop to 16% this year. Below, 2012 tax rates.

Pfizer		29%
Gilead		27
Biogen Idec		25
Merck		24
Bristol-Myers		**23**
Lilly		23
Amgen		16
Celgene		16

Note: Non-GAAP rate
Source: ISI Group   The Wall Street Journal

in the U.S., but in practice, much of that cash is banked in the U.S."

This chart comes from the Wall Street Journal story on the shuffling of sales abroad for big drug firms who are attempting to avoid the punitive tax rate of 20% or higher by shifting revenue overseas.

Do you have the right legal structure?
When we take a look at how your business is structured, I will challenge the concept of an S corporation vs. a C corporation. ("S" and "C" refer to subchapters of the IRS Code that contains the rules and regulations related to the taxation of corporations.)

My experience dictates that generally it is better to have privately-held companies taxed as S-Corps. rather than C-Corps.

As discussed earlier, the profits of an S corporation are passed through to the shareholders' personal income tax returns and therefore are taxed at the owner's marginal tax rate.

A C corporation is what I refer to as a traditional corporation. It is an entity that is separate from its shareholders and it pays its own income taxes. My experience dictates that generally it is better to have privately-held companies taxed as S-Corps. rather than C-Corps.

However, to take advantage of the benefits of the **Kissling Tax Method™**, most often, my clients find it beneficial to have a combination of both S-Corps. and C-Corps.

TACTIC #4: Captive Insurance Company.
The term "captive" was coined by the "father of captive insurance," Frederic M. Reiss, while he was bringing his concept into practice for his first client, the Youngstown Sheet & Tube Company ("Company"), in Ohio in the 1950's. The Company had a series of mining operations. Its management referred to the mines, whose output was put solely to the corporation's use, as "captive mines."

When Reiss helped the Company incorporate its own insurance subsidiaries, they were referred to as "captive insurance companies" because they wrote insurance exclusively for the "captive mines." Reiss continued to use the term because in this tactic, the policyholder owned the insurance company, i.e. the insurer was "captive" to the policyholder. Today, there are over 5,000 captive insurance companies.

Reiss continued to use the term because in this tactic, the policyholder owns the insurance company i.e. the insurer is "captive" to the policyholder.

The reason for Youngstown Sheet and Tube Company to create its own insurance company was profit motivated.

Their risk managers concluded that the Company had some financial risk related to its "captive mines" and they needed to set aside a certain amount of money to cover future liabilities should they arise.

If liability did not arise, Youngstown Sheet and Tube Company would keep the associated profits from its captive insurance company, rather giving those profits to a third party insurance company.

The Company must not have thought that the risk was so high that they would want to transfer the risk to an unrelated insurance company as they did with their normal property and casualty risks.

If you are pondering this process, you may be thinking: why wouldn't management just have set funds in a reserve account? Doing so would have allowed the Company to have the funds available in the event of a claim. And, it would not need to incur all of the cost of creating and maintaining another company.

The answer to your question is: the reason for creating the captive insurance company was to save income taxes.

When an operating company writes a check to purchase the insurance, it receives a tax deduction. It is similar to buying your liability insurance from a third party insurance company. But the beautiful thing about a captive insurance company is that the revenue received by the insurance company is not taxable to the insurance company, as long as the participants follow all of the rules.

Summary of Captive Insurance Companies.
If the operating company sets up a reserve account to handle future claims, it is not permitted to take a tax deduction until a claim is made. If a claim is never made, the company never incurs the expense.

If we set up a captive insurance company, we get a tax deduction in the current year on the operating company's tax return. And, we do not pay taxes on the funds received by the insurance company.

At a minimum, we have created an advantageous tax-deferral. If handled properly, the earnings from the insurance company can remain tax-free.

At a minimum, we have created an advantageous tax deferral. If handled properly, the earnings from the insurance company can be returned on a tax-free basis. This is what we were talking about in Chapter 5. It creates a tax deduction today and a chance at taking those funds back later, maybe at retirement, on a tax-free basis.

It is important that you realize that there are many rules and regulations related to captive insurance companies. The rules are set by both the IRS and by local insurance regulators. If you qualify and follow the rules properly, the tax benefits can be substantial.

TACTIC #5: Over-funded Cash Value Life Insurance.

There is a tool available for tax-free retirement that many simply overlook. However, it is one of the most powerful tools available for creating and guarding wealth in retirement.

It's called an over-funded cash value life insurance policy. There are several types of life insurance that qualify as "cash value." Whole life, universal life, variable life, and indexed life are all cash value life insurance policies.

We will use universal life insurance (UL) only for our discussion. even though the method is available using any cash value type of insurance product..

According to NAIC (National Association of Insurance Commissioners), a UL allows the policyholder to: determine the amount and timing of premium payments within certain limits as set by the IRS (more often than not, things that are good are limited by the IRS); and to adjust coverage levels as the policy owner's needs change. It includes guaranteed, annual cash value growth, among other benefits.
Under the terms of the policy, the excess of premium payments above the current cost of insurance is credited to the cash value of the policy.

The cash value is credited each month with interest, and the policy is debited each month by a cost of insurance (COI) charge, as well as any other policy charges and fees which are drawn from the cash value, even if no premium payment is made that month.

Living Benefits of Life Insurance.

Without getting into all details, I want to emphasize that life insurance has many benefits for the living policy owner, as opposed to only being a death benefit provided to the beneficiary.

Some of these benefits include loans, withdrawals, collateral assignments, split dollar agreements, pension funding, and tax planning.

> *Some of these benefits include loans, withdrawals, collateral assignments, split dollar agreements, pension funding, and tax planning.*

The Loan Benefit.

Most cash value life insurance policies come with an option to take a loan on certain values associated with the policy. What most people do not understand is that the loan is actually from the insurance company, with your insurance policy acting as the collateral against the amount borrowed. Thus, the cash value of the insurance policy remains in tack and will continue to earn an interest, or investment, return during the loan period.

From a taxation perspective a business owner knows that money received from a loan is not a taxable event. There is no income tax on borrowed money. Thus, if you borrow against your cash value you could create an income pool that is not subject to taxation.

Repayment of the loan principal is not required on an annual basis, but payment of the loan interest is required. If the loan interest is not paid, it will be deducted from the cash value of the policy. If there is not sufficient value left in the policy to cover interest, the policy simply lapses. (Consult a CPA or financial professional before allowing a policy to lapse. If you have taken loans against the policy you could have income tax implications.)

Loans are not reported to any credit agency and payment and non-payment against them will not affect the policyholder's credit rating. If the policy has not become a "modified endowment," the loans are withdrawn from the policy values from the premium first, then from gains.

The loans do need to be paid back to the insurance company upon death. Outstanding loans are deducted from the death benefit at the death of the insured.

The Tax-free Advantage of Loans.
According to the insurance industry regulatory body, if the policy is set up, funded and distributed properly, and according to IRS regulations, an equity indexed UL policy will provide an investor with many years of tax-free income.

Another advantage is that tax-free withdrawals can be made through internal policy loans.

"This can significantly outperform traditional investments such as stocks, bonds, mutual funds, CD's or annuities that are placed in taxable and tax-deferred accounts such as an IRA, 401K . . ."

I find it interesting that even the regulatory agencies and insurance experts will assert this benefit.

To summarize, you contribute to your life insurance policy, but you do not get an income tax deduction. When appropriate, you can borrow against the policy without triggering a taxable event. Thus, you can have a tax-free retirement.

In this chapter I've shared with you a few of the tactics available in the **Kissling Tax Method™**. Now you can see that there are many tools to utilize in planning a tax-free retirement. Why wouldn't you take advantage of these methods?

Once again, I have to ask you:

> *If your tax attorney or CPA isn't approaching your goals and needs this way, and isn't asking some of these same questions, you need to ask yourself, "Why?"*

> "If you don't design your own life plan, chances are you'll fall into someone else's plan. And guess what they have planned for you? Not much." **Jim Rohn**

The Fine Art of Estate Planning

The frightening reality is that if you die unexpectedly without an estate plan, your family could lose over 40% of your assets in a flash. **TK.**

The estate plan is the plan everyone wants to avoid. It forces the individual to realize his or her own mortality. It is a reminder that life on Earth is not forever and the race will, at some point, come to an end.

When considering estate planning, you must cope with very personal questions on physical, spiritual and financial levels. Sometimes it is uncomfortable, but for the sake of your survivors, these issues must be addressed sooner rather than later.

If you view your family tree in terms of multiple generations, each lifetime is actually very short.

The principal cause of estate planning procrastination is the fact that most people believe they only need to deal with it when they reach old age. For the most part, that is true.

When considering estate planning, you must cope with many very personal questions on physical, spiritual and financial levels.

However, since we don't know exactly when we are going to die, we aren't aware of just how "old" we are, relatively speaking. In other words, if you pass away at age 26, you were old at age 25.

My point is, if you want to take care of your family for generations to come, you must have a plan in order now. The frightening reality is that if you die unexpectedly, without an estate plan, your family could lose over 40% of your assets in a flash.

At a major convention in the summer of 2012, I was invited to speak on topics related to the anticipated changes to the federal income tax laws. I spent most of the time talking about the new tax rates.

I spoke about how there were going to be tax increases on everyone, and that there would be increases in taxes related to Obamacare.

One of the big topics at the time concerned what was going to happen to the federal inheritance tax.

This is when I coined the concept **"Think Beyond Now™."**

Remember, back in the summer of 2012, we were near the expiration of the Bush Era tax breaks. This meant that the exemption from the federal inheritance tax would have been reduced to $1,000,000 per person and millions of Americans would become subject to the federal inheritance tax upon their death.

During the convention in 2012, I coined the concept **"Think Beyond Now™."** I told the members of the audience that they ought to take their heads out of the sand and focus on their financial future because they could work their entire lives to become financially successful only to give half of it to the federal government upon their deaths.

I love my country, but I love my kids more, and I don't want to give my hard earned assets to the government at their expense.

In the fall of 2012, I spent a great deal of time with my clients, shifting ownership of assets to their children and grandchildren. In many cases, we set up trusts and family limited partnerships. We also took advantage of the many different financial vehicles I've told you about in the previous chapter in an effort to minimize the size of their estates in anticipation of the big change that was coming.

Then, in December 2012, our Congress and President got together and passed "The American Taxpayer Relief Act of 2012."

This legislation caught most tax professionals off guard in the area of estate planning. Instead of the exemption amount being reduced to $1,000,000 per person it was increased to $5,000,000 per person and is now indexed to inflation.

Consequently, in 2013, the new federal exemption amount came to be $5,250,000 per person. Furthermore, the tax rate that was on target to move back up to 55% of an estate's value was moved to 40%.

> *They couldn't imagine their estates ever breaking $5,000,000, plus the adjustments for inflation.*

All of a sudden it appeared that federal estate taxes were no longer going to be as big of a concern.

When these changes took place, millions of taxpayers were removed from the list of those who would potentially pay federal inheritance taxes. Frankly, a very small percentage of the United States population have estates valued over $5,000,000.

Many of my friends, clients, and colleagues were relieved to think that they would no longer need to be concerned about estate planning. They couldn't imagine their estates ever breaking $5,000,000, plus the adjustments for inflation.

This is when I reminded them that they needed to **Think Beyond Now™!** We need to think beyond the simple and obvious!

When I get involved with my clients' finances, I feel it is my responsibility to focus on the weaknesses in their plans and the areas they are not addressing. Let's face it: a plan is only as good as its weakest link! If we take our eye off the ball, we are sure to get hurt.

The first thing I want to remind you is that just because the federal government is willing to increase the exemption level to $5,000,000, that does not mean that your specific state is willing to increase the exemption level.

Following are a couple of examples:

---⬥---

Pennsylvania.

Recently, a client of mine who had a net estate value of $2,000,000 passed away. At this value, his estate was not subject to federal inheritance tax, and the heirs did not have to pay any taxes to the federal government. However, this client passed away in the state of Pennsylvania.

Pennsylvania does not have an inheritance tax exemption amount. In fact, many states do not have exemption amounts. Some have very low exemption amounts.

In Pennsylvania there is a flat tax on estates. The rate is determined by to whom the assets are being passed. If the funds are being passed to your children, the rate is 4.5%. In this case the tax would be $90,000.

> *If the funds are being passed to your children, the rate is 4.5%. In this case the tax would be $90,000.*

However, because this client did not have children, he left his assets to his nieces, so his estate was taxed at the rate of 15%, or $300,000.

Is this reason enough for you to do some estate planning in an effort to mitigate tax? I would think so.

---⬥---

Florida.

Florida does not have either an income tax or an estate tax. From a taxation perspective alone, Florida is a good state in which both to live and die. If your estate is expected to be less than the federal exemption, your heirs can expect to not pay any inheritance tax.

However, there is more to the Florida tax story. Clients of mine are residents of the state of Florida with current assets below the federal exemption amount. I recently met with them, and discovered that when "Grandpa" sold the family farm in North Dakota in 1960, he retained the mineral rights to the property.

Now, some 50+ years later, there is a probability that the property has oil on it, so the couple in Florida could receive royalty checks in the future from mineral rights in North Dakota that they only recently discovered that they owned.

These royalties could be over $500,000 per year.

All of a sudden, these clients have two major estate tax issues:

> 1. *There is a possibility that if an oil company drills on the property and hits oil, their estate could very well be worth more than $5,250,000. Thus, they could be subject to the federal inheritance tax.*
> 2. *The property is located in North Dakota. Even though this couple lives in Florida they are liable for the estate taxes in the state where the assets are held. Consequently, they would be subject to North Dakota estate*

> *taxes. (Note: luckily for this couple, North Dakota currently **does not** have an estate or inheritance tax. My point is, you can be subject to an estate or inheritance tax in a state other than where you are a resident.)*
>
> *In this case, my solution for my clients was for them to gift these mineral rights to the next generation before the rights become even more valuable.*

At this point, it is important that I take a moment to explain a few general points about state inheritance and estate taxes.

I use the terms "inheritance tax" and "estate tax" interchangeably, because they are both a tax on the value of a person's assets upon his or her death. However, these concepts are legally different.

> **An estate tax is paid by the estate.**
>
> **An inheritance tax is paid by the beneficiary.**

Some states have an estate tax and some have an inheritance tax, some have both, and many do not have either.

It is crucial that you find out if the state in which you live has a death tax of some kind or another. If you are lucky enough to not to have a death tax in your state, and if you manage to keep your estate value below the federal exemption amount, you do not need to be concerned about a tax upon your death.

To summarize the issue: if you have an estate with a net asset value of less than $5,250,000 and your state does not have an estate tax, you do not need to be concerned about estate taxes.

If your state does have an estate tax, then you should take the time to decide if the potential tax is significant enough to justify the cost of planning your estate.

> *The **Kissling Tax Method**™ is about building wealth, not just for the current generation, but also for generations to come.*

If your estate value is greater than $5,250,000, then you need to get your head out of the sand and devise a plan to pass your assets to your children as efficiently as possible.

As I guide my clients to **Think Beyond Now**™, I encourage them to realize that successful businesspersons build enough wealth to support their families for several generations. The **Kissling Tax Method**™ is about building wealth, not just for the current generation, but also for generations to come.

Let's look at a few strategies to help us pass value to our children.

STRATEGY 1: Family Limited Partnerships.
I have been a big fan of the family limited partnership for a very long time. The reason that I am a big supporter of the concept is that it is a way to control assets, and, it is more important to control assets than to own them.

The term "family" limited partnership merely indicates that the owners of a particular limited partnership are all members of your family. The actual legal structure is the same as any other limited partnership.

———— ❦ ————

About 15 years ago, very dear friends of mine, Dan and Rachel, purchased a piece of real estate. The husband is a bit of a real estate junkie and thought it would be nice to own this particular parcel of farmland. They bought it as a long-term investment. Dan thought perhaps it would act as a hedge against inflation. They knew that there was a good chance that they would pass the property to their children and grandchildren.

At the time of the purchase, I recommended that my friends consider placing the land inside a family limited partnership. Dan and Rachel gave each of their four children 10% of the company, or essentially 40% of the land. But what they did not give their children was any rights to control the land. That is because the children are limited partners, and Dan and his wife are the general partners. The general partners make all of the rules. Dan, like me, likes to remind his kids that they have no rights.

> **The general partners make all of the rules.**

When we started the partnership, Dan and Rachel's children's ages ranged from four to 15. They had many concerns about turning assets over to them. First, whom would they marry? What if a child's spouse turned out to be a creep that they didn't like? What if one of their children ended up with a divorce? Would they then have the possibility of a non-family member as a limited partner? Another big issue was that at these young ages, Dan and Rachel's children did not have the maturity to handle financial decisions.

There are pros and cons with family limited

partnerships, as with any financial tool, so you need to make sure the tool fits your need. All the details of the ins and outs of a family limited partnership are beyond the scope of our discussion here. I suggest that before you conclude that it is the best tool for your situation, consult with a good CPA and/or tax attorney.

I really like the fact that with a family limited partnership, you can pass on a lot of assets at discounted rates and you can keep control of the assets. Further, a family limited partnership is a good way to protect assets from a limited liability perspective.

In my opinion, the best assets to pass on to the next generation are those assets that are expected to appreciate and assets that you are not anticipating needing for the life-long welfare of you and your spouse. The best time to contribute, or gift, the asset is when the assets is at its lowest value. Typically, that is when the asset is purchased.

> *. . . as this land appreciates in value, the increase will now grow at 60% to the parents' estate and 40% to the children's estate.*

Let's walk through Dan and Rachel's farmland case. They purchased the land for about $300,000. As purchasers, they contributed a down payment of $60,000 and took out a mortgage of $240,000. Since they gave their children a total of 40% of the family limited partnership, they gifted a $24,000 ($60,000 x 40%)

value to their children and were not required to file a gift tax return. (A gift tax return is required to be filed anytime an individual gifts more than $13,000 of value to another individual.)

Dan and Rachel accomplished the following: as the land appreciates in value, the increase will grow at 60% to the parents' estate and 40% to the children's estate. What has happened with this land? Not much so far. Dan and Rachel have rented it each year to a farmer to help pay some of the real estate taxes. And the mortgage is paid down a little bit each year.

> *There is a very good chance that the land will be worth millions of dollars in the future.*

A more recent development in the story is the discovery of a significant amount of natural gas under Dan and Rachel's property.

Major oil companies have started leasing large sections of land in the local area for the purpose of drilling for natural gas. Now Dan and Rachel could possibly sell the land for double the purchase price.

There is a very good chance that the land will be worth millions of dollars in the future. The expected value now is well beyond the expectations of the value of the property when my friends purchased it. Only time will tell . . . but that is my point.

You don't know what is going to happen in the future. That is why I recommend transferring assets sooner rather than later. Dan and Rachel were a little leery about transferring 40% of their property to their children 15 years ago. Now they are quickly trying

Assuming that my clients' assets are over the federal estate tax limit, this move just saved the kids $900,000 in federal estate taxes on a merely 40% ownership.

to transfer more to them while values are still relatively low!

Based upon the potential value of the natural gas on Dan and Rachel's property, there is a chance that the real estate could be worth $5 million once the drilling takes place. Assuming that my clients' assets are over the federal estate tax limit, establishing a family limited partnership saved the kids $900,000 in federal estate taxes on merely 40% ownership.

At some time we will all get older and our mental capacity will begin to slip. By that time, we can assume that one of our children will have taken an interest and will be willing to become involved in the management of the family's assets.

Then the partners can get together and elect a new general partner. At that point, one of the children will become the manager (general partner) and the parents will become limited partners. This, too, has advantages from an estate tax perspective.

Let me explain. Upon the death of the parents, the executor of the estate will need to have all of the assets appraised and valued as of the date of death. Some of this process is easy. For example, if the estate has marketable securities you can look up the security's value at market closing on the date of death.

——— ✺ ———

If you have a family limited partnership in which you are a limited partner, the process will involve you engaging a professional appraiser. The real estate appraiser will go through the normal process and place a value on the real estate owned by the partnership. Then the value is allocated by the percentage of ownership.

At a tax rate of 40%, this is a tax savings of $600,000.

However, the value attributed to the limited partner would be further discounted, in accordance with IRS regulations, because the limited partner does not have the right to make the decision to liquidate his assets. That means there is a limited market for the asset. The discount could be as high as 50% of the value.

Returning to the story of the parcel of farm land:

> Let's assume that the land is worth $5 million upon the death of the second spouse and that Dan and Rachel had maintained 60% ownership in the partnership. However, they did become limited partners three years prior to death. Upon their deaths, the 60% ownership would be worth $3 million. Nevertheless, since they were limited partners, the value could be further discounted another $1.5 million. So, they would pass an asset worth $3 million to the children at a taxable value of $1.5 million. At a tax rate of 40%, this is a tax savings of $600,000. This is in addition to the $900,000 saved by transferring 40% of the value to the children when the real estate was first purchased.

——— ✺ ———

Dan and Rachel's experience is a very compelling story to support the use of a family limited partnership. It is a great tool that I have used for my clients on many occasions. But, always consult with a professional to determine if it is appropriate for you.

STRATEGY 2: Irrevocable Trust.
An irrevocable trust is another good tool to consider when you are looking to pass appreciating assets to the next generation in an estate-tax efficient manner. Just like the family limited partnership, any assets that are contributed to the trust become the property of the trust and are no longer a part of the estate.

> *In the case of a trust, you can lose control of the management decisions while you are alive. But, you can control the assets after your death.*

The big difference between the family limited partnership and an irrevocable trust is control.

While you can contribute assets to a family limited partnership and still maintain control of the underlying assets while you are alive, you lose control upon your death. In the case of a trust, you can lose control of the management decisions while you are alive. But, you can control the assets after your death. All of the control is passed to the Trustee and the Trustee must manage the trust purely in accordance with the trust agreement.

Since the trust is irrevocable, it is imperative to be very careful in drafting the trust document. Once the document is signed, it is carved in stone and cannot be changed. It takes a court order to change a trust document and most courts are hesitant to allow changes.

Let's use the same example used above. What would the results have been if during Dan and Rachel's lifetime they had contributed the land to a trust rather than a family limited partnership? The trust could have been set up so the kids would receive 40% of the income and the parents would receive 60% of the income. Upon Dan and Rachel's deaths, none of the real estate would have been subject to estate taxes. Just like the family limited partnership.

However, the Trustee would have had control of management decisions related to whether or not to sign a lease with an oil company or whether to develop the property. The trustee could have decided that it was in the best interest of the beneficiaries to sell the land before the natural gas was discovered. Selling would have saved the estate taxes, but would have lost management control.   In this scenario, the flexibility of the family limited partnership trumps the benefit of the irrevocable trust.

Sometimes the loss of management control is an acceptable tradeoff. I find that most people like the irrevocable trust because they can control their assets to a certain extent after death. Many parents rightly believe that if their children inherit a bunch of money the children are not prepared to handle the money. So the parents want to set up parameters controlling the flow of money to their children.

Many times parents will set up a trust that limits the flow of income to their children until a certain age, such as age 30. If parents are concerned that their children will have trouble maintaining employment, they may set up a provision stating that a child is not allowed a distribution greater than earnings for employment. So, if the child does not work, he is not entitled to a distribution from the trust.

If you and your attorney take the time to properly develop your trust document, you will be able to control your assets after death. In the case of the family limited partnership, upon your death, your children already own their share of the assets without limitation related to the distribution of income.

The bottom line is that the both family limited partnership and the irrevocable trust are good estate planning tools. But, both have their pro's and con's.

Remember Joe?
Do you recall the list of tactics I set up for Joe, back in Chapter 3? The last three items on the list are especially aggressive vehicles for a tax-free retirement and for wealth transfer.

They are: Closely Held Insurance Company; Non-qualified Investments; and U.S. Possession Companies that are profitable and will be available to support Joe's retirement in the future.

These are some of the most aggressive, smart and legal vehicles available to us for generating a tax-free retirement and for efficiently transferring assets to the next generation.

Closely Held Insurance Company (CHIC)
Following is an example of how CHIC works as a

wealth transfer vehicle. With a net worth of over $5 million, and a company that earned more than $1 million per year, Joe decided he needed to transfer some of his assets to his children. At the time, he was 50-something, married with children and owned his company.

Remember, the CHIC was originally owned solely by Joe. It was first set up as a method to protect Joe's company against a real, potential legal liability. If the liability was not incurred by the company, the insurance company would then be more profitable. Those profits, if properly handled, would be available to Joe as a tax-efficient retirement plan.

It turned out that Joe did not need the assets for his retirement. As soon as he concluded that he would not need the insurance company he gifted the stock to an irrevocable trust that granted him the right to the income from the trust during his life. The principal would transfer to his children upon his death.

If you review this case you will see that the CHIC was a legal protection asset until its purpose changed. Then it became a tax-free retirement vehicle, until the need was no longer there. Then, by gifting it to the trust, it became a tax-efficient tool to pass assets to his children.

Non-qualified Investments.
For Joe and his wife, they can deposit as much as they want into their non-qualified investment plan, once they have paid earning taxes on the money. Some of the benefits of this strategy are: accessibility; and

the fact that, due to the lower tax rates or long-term capital gains, an investor often will pay less on a non-qualified investment than on qualified earnings.

> *As I have said many times, you cannot control your results if you don't have a plan.*

I advise you to analyze the tools and utilize them to their best effect. When I work with my clients on estate planning, sometimes we use one tool or the other, but there are many times when we use several.

Often we set up a family limited partnership and then we contribute the limited partnership interest to the irrevocable trust and hold the general partnership interest outside the trust.

As a result, my clients can still have management control while moving a significant portion of the assets into a trust so that they can still control the flow of income to their children after their death.

I cannot emphasis enough the need for estate planning. As I have said many times, you cannot control your results if you don't have a plan.

Over the span of my career, I have found that of all taxes, the estate tax is generally the most controllable.

With an adept guide, you can take the proper steps to minimize this

> *"I think we need a very, very serious effort, primarily through tax policy to provide incentives and encouragement for people to save and invest and expand their businesses and to create more jobs. The kind of thing we did in the early Reagan years, 30 years ago. I think that's essential."* **Dick Cheney**